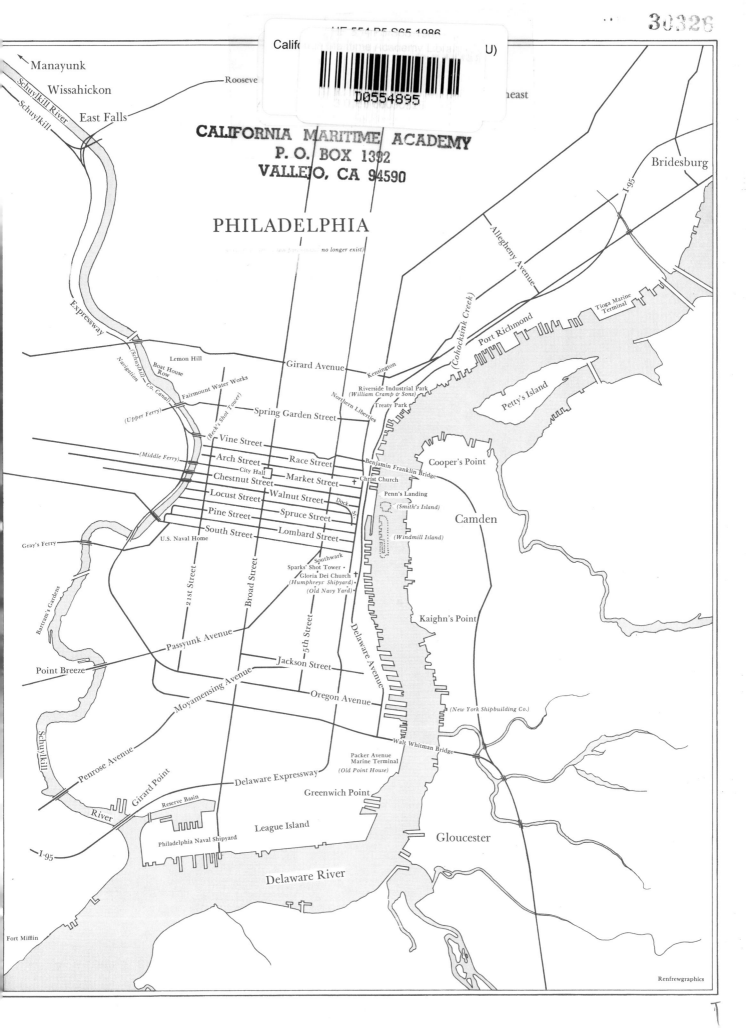

30326

CALIFORNIA MARITIME ACADEMY
P. O. BOX 1392
VALLEJO, CA 94590

D0554895

Philadelphia on the River

PHILADELPHIA MARITIME MUSEUM · 1986

DISTRIBUTED BY THE UNIVERSITY OF PENNSYLVANIA PRESS

LIBRARY
CALIFORNIA MARITIME ACADEMY
P. O. BOX 1392
VALLEJO, CA 94590

3·326

PHILIP CHADWICK FOSTER SMITH

PHILADELPHIA WITHDRAWN
ON THE RIVER

OTHER BOOKS BY PHILIP C. F. SMITH

A History of the Marine Society at Salem in New-England, 1766-1966 (1966)
Portraits of the Marine Society at Salem in New-England (1972)
The Frigate *Essex* Papers: Building the Salem Frigate, 1798-1799 (1974)
Captain Samuel Tucker (1747-1833), Continental Navy (1976)
Fired by Manley Zeal: A Naval Fiasco of the American Revolution (1977)
The Artful Roux, Marine Painters of Marseille (1978)
More Marine Paintings and Drawings in the Peabody Museum (1979)
The *Empress of China* (1984)

BOOKS EDITED BY PHILIP C. F. SMITH

The Journals of Ashley Bowen (1728-1813) of Marblehead (2 vols.) (1973)
Mowee: An Informal History of the Hawaiian Island
    by Cummins E. Speakman, Jr. (1978)
Seafaring in Colonial Massachusetts (1980)
Sibley's Heir, A Volume in Memory of Clifford Kenyon Shipton (1982)

TITLE PAGE:
A detail from a painting by A. Staehle illustrates the Philadelphia waterfront
in 1881. See Figure 35. *(Philadelphia Maritime Museum: Loan from the J. Welles
Henderson Collection)*

Copyright © 1986 by the Philadelphia Maritime Museum
Library of Congress Catalogue Card Number: 85-060100
I.S.B.N. 0-913346-10-1

Designed by Klaus Gemming, New Haven, Connecticut
Composition by Finn Typographic Service, Stamford, Connecticut
Printing by Meriden-Stinehour Press, Meriden, Connecticut
Binding by Meriden-Stinehour Press, Lunenburg, Vermont

To J. WELLES HENDERSON
Lifelong Student of the Bay and River Delaware
and Founder of the Philadelphia Maritime Museum

FOREWORD

PHILADELPHIA, some say, is one of the most liveable cities in the United States. Many of its Center City and suburban inhabitants would agree, yet on that subject relatively few would be inclined towards public oratory. "Penn's Towne" could well be one of America's best kept secrets, and many Philadelphians like to keep it that way.

Tourist Philadelphia evokes such conventional images as Independence Hall, the Liberty Bell, Benjamin Franklin, the Betsy Ross House, The Philadelphia Museum of Art, the Pennsylvania Academy of the Fine Arts, and enough other noteworthy attractions to keep an out-of-towner on the run for weeks on end without pausing for breath.

All these visions, and many more, are interwoven into the mental costume Philadelphians wear in perception of themselves. From the Phillies, the Radnor Races, the annual Mummers' Parade, and the Eagles to the Sixers, the Devon Horse Show, First City Troop Balls, and the Rittenhouse Square Flower Market, a hundred thousand emotional pictures complete the fabric of the city's social and commercial life.

One image is so conspicuous as to be blinding. And blind to it the majority of Philadelphians seem to be. Philadelphia is a major port city – and has been for more than three hundred years.

As for out-of-towners: well, the City of Brotherly Love simply does not naturally elicit the contemplation of global maritime commerce or of an unique shipping history. Kuwait, London, New York, Rotterdam, Singapore: yes. Baltimore, Bombay, Boston, San Francisco, Stockholm: maybe. But, Philadelphia? Absolutely, not!

Wrong.

This volume invites disbelievers to discover Philadelphia's ubiquitous waterfront as it has evolved during the past two centuries since colonial days. Only a nostalgic peep can be offered, however, because the subjects worthy of inclusion are so abundant, so rich, and the views so virtually inexhaustible that no single endeavor could do any one of them justice. The book is therefore presented as an hors d'oeuvre to whet the appetite for a banquet yet to be served, perceived eventually to become an open-ended monograph series of separate offerings, each one carefully seasoned to accent its individual characteristics.

A great many subtle and insidious changes have engulfed maritime Philadelphia during these two hundred years. Steam replaced sail; the whispery flow of petroleum silenced the rumble of coal, bridges sent ferries to the breakers' yards; climatic modifications and industrial effluvia in the water and air broke the cycle of ice-choked rivers in wintertime. Mobility on land provoked the demise of the day-liners and excursion steamers which once plied the Delaware River with efficient regularity as well as coastwise passenger and freight lines. Air travel forced transoceanic passenger liners out of business. The agricultural exports of the early days gave way to the goods and machinery of the Industrial Age, which in their turns, were replaced by the esoteric productions of the Technological Era. And shipbuilding—once so pervasive an industry between Wilmington and Philadelphia that the Delaware came to be called the "American Clyde"—has all but disappeared from the scene.

So, too, has the daily sight of large numbers of towering ships being warped into their berths alongside the piers of downtown Delaware Avenue. Following a worldwide tendency, exemplified by such ports as London and Rotterdam, today's mammoth supertankers, container ships, and roll-on/ roll-off (ro-ro) vessels are tending to load and discharge cargoes further and further away from the city's traditional business core.

On a thirty-nine-acre site along South Delaware Avenue, from South Street north to Market, an area once occupied by more than a dozen active piers, is now the public-oriented Penn's Landing, planned for recreational, service, business, and commercial uses, all adjacent to its extensive pleasure boat basin and residential condominiums nearby. As the years pass, it is probable that public use of the riverfront will expand both upriver and down. But here is the germ of an ironic dichotomy.

As more and more people flock to Philadelphia's future waterfront attractions, the fewer will be the sights and sounds of maritime commerce in the vicinity and the lesser will be the public's perception of Philadelphia as a continuing port of international proportions.

Not all that many years ago, even well after completion of the suspension bridge linking Philadelphia and Camden, ferries still swam like water beetles across the stretch of river where once alluvial islands with baths and beer gardens had attracted a nineteenth-century populace. Rust-streaked tramp steamers churned by, propellor blades turning slowly and just breaking the surface as brawny little tugs with tall funnels belching smoke hauled strings of barges upriver or an aged four-masted schooner down. Horses and drays, and then motorized trucks, clattered and spluttered over the Belgian block paving of Delaware Avenue, while steam switching engines pushed long freights into the piers lining it. No one observing such a scene could possibly doubt that Philadelphia was a great port. Yet, the sights and sounds and scents of the similar, modern maritime environment have almost crept away beyond the range of the ordinary tourist and average Philadelphian.

The illustrations selected for this book are intended to resurrect in the mind's eye of the present day the ambience of past times, long erased. They have been culled from many thousands observed in public archives and private collections. Some are familiar from earlier publications; many are not. Some are unique; others are less so; perhaps in some cases better ones might have been found had more time been available to comb every conceivable source, yet each strives to contribute to an understanding of what has so often been overlooked in Philadelphia's luxuriant history—its circumferential waterways.

Many of the pictures, but by no means all, have been drawn from the collections of the Philadelphia Maritime Museum. Many hundred views, from its print, painting, and photographic archives still await special subject publication. How they came to be amassed in the first place relates to the reason for the issuance of this book.

Among the few Philadelphians of the present era who looked first and foremost towards the Delaware River and, even as a youth, had begun to gather the physical remembrances of its maritime strength, must be named J. Welles Henderson, Esq., an attorney and the son of one of the country's late preeminent admiralty lawyers.

During the summer of 1957, Henderson's ever-growing collection was exhibited not in Philadelphia, where it was then neither widely known nor appreciated (despite a small display mounted two years earlier in The Athenaeum of Philadelphia), but at the Peabody Museum of Salem, Massachusetts, a venerable institution founded in 1799 and largely devoted to American maritime history.

The exhibition was so well received in Salem that The Free Library of Philadelphia was moved to repeat it some months later. The encouragement engendered by the success of these occasions thus prompted Welles Henderson to found the Philadelphia Maritime Museum in 1960. The initial displays were formally opened to the public on 19 May 1961 in a rented room at The Athenaeum, from which it eventually moved to larger rented quarters, and, finally, in 1974, to a building of its own at 321 Chestnut Street, directly opposite Carpenters' Hall in Independence Park.

Publication of *Philadelphia on the River,* therefore, marks the twenty-fifth anniversary year since the Philadelphia Maritime Museum's formal opening. That it does is a happy reason to put forward a lasting tribute to maritime Philadelphia and to those who preserve the memories of its past.

To the Andrew W. Mellon Foundation, which provided the grant supporting this publication, the Philadelphia Maritime Museum, as well as the undersigned, express their grateful acknowledgements.

PHILIP CHADWICK FOSTER SMITH

Bath, Maine
October 1985

ACKNOWLEDGEMENTS

For their willing assistance, I most gratefully thank J. Welles Henderson, Chairman of the Philadelphia Maritime Museum's Board of Port Wardens; Theodore T. Newbold, the Museum's President; Jane E. Allen, Acting Curator; Roger B. Allen, Curator of Watercraft; Dorothy H. Mueller, Librarian; Mary Beth Reed, lately Curatorial Assistant; as well as Stanhope S. Browne, Esq.; Mrs. Joseph Carson; Gerald M. Cope; Paul Karnow; James E. Mooney; L. Rodman Page; Mrs. Lawrence M.C. Smith; and S. Robert Teitelman, Esq.

Also, Georgia B. Bumgardner, American Antiquarian Society, Worcester, Massachusetts; Roy E. Goodman, American Philosophical Society, Philadelphia; Sandra Gross, Atwater Kent Museum, Philadelphia; Miriam Favorite, Camden County Historical Society, Camden, New Jersey; Ward J. Childs, City Archives of Philadelphia; Delbert R. Gutridge, Cleveland Museum of Art; Rowland Elzea, Delaware Art Museum, Wilmington; Dr. Robert F. Looney, Free Library of Philadelphia; Linda Stanley, Historical Society of Pennsylvania, Philadelphia; Kenneth Finkel, Library Company of Philadelphia; John S. Carter, Maine Maritime Museum, Bath, Maine; John O. Sands and Lois Oglesby, Mariner's Museum, Newport News, Virginia; Benjamin A. G. Fuller and Richard C. Malley, Mystic Seaport Museum, Mystic, Connecticut; Gary A. Reynolds, Newark Museum, Newark, New Jersey; Kathy Flynn and Paul F. Johnston, Peabody Museum of Salem, Salem, Massachusetts; Frank Goodyear and Robert Arthur Harman, The Pennsylvania Academy of the Fine Arts, Philadelphia; Darrell L. Sewall, The Philadelphia Museum of Art; Nancy S. Gaylord, Philadelphia Port Corporation; and John H. Braunlein, Rockwood Museum, Wilmington, Delaware.

It was again a pleasure to work closely with Klaus Gemming, whose design work is always as inspired as his production supervision is impeccable.

My wife, Meredith, has not only my thanks but also deserves that of readers. She dissected draft upon draft to search out and attempt to destroy those myriad, convoluted phrases which, in her judgement, were intelligible only to me. For that, and so much more, goes my deepest gratitude.

P.C.F.S.

Philadelphia on the River

1. THE SAND HILLS of Cape Henlopen, Delaware, and Cape May, New Jersey, flank the approaches to Delaware Bay and the broad river of the same name that has its sources in the Catskill Mountains some 280 miles to the north. Neither Cape rises majestically from the sea to warn inward-bound navigators of its presence, so upon each has been built a lighthouse to guide the unsuspecting mariner. The mid-to-late-nineteenth-century Philadelphia artist David J. Kennedy depicted an outsized pilot schooner with a southeasterly breeze and a steamer cruising the bay beyond Cape Henlopen Light, the seventh to be built in North America. Constructed upon a sandy hogback and first illuminated in 1767, the British burned the tower during the American Revolution, but it was restored to operation in 1784 and remained in use until perpetually shifting dunes ultimately undermined its foundations. The light collapsed onto the beach about 1 PM on 13 April 1926. It has since been replaced by another in a more secure position. *(Historical Society of Pennsylvania)*

1

Ang.5ᵗʰ.1841.   Lighthouses at Lewistown Delᵉ

2

2. GERMAN-BORN Philadelphia artist Augustus Kollner sketched the 126-foot-high Cape Henlopen Light and its little brother beacon on 5 August 1841. Judging by the windbreak shored up against the windward side of the hogback, site erosion had already become a problem. The forty-five-foot stone beacon, erected in 1825, stood three-quarters of a mile north of the main lighthouse. For twenty years, one keeper serviced both, an exhausting job at best and next to impossible when wintry midnight gales lashed the barren Cape sands. Shifting dunes prompted the building of a new beacon in 1864-1865 and the old one to be taken down. The light-keeper's cottage appears not too snugly nestled against the hummock behind the octagonal, whitewashed tower. The dangling rope no doubt helped the keeper to haul the light's whale oil fuel to its lofty reservoir. *(Delaware Art Museum: Samuel and Mary R. Bancroft Collection)*

3. CAPE MAY, New Jersey, thrusts itself out into Delaware Bay some twelve-and-a-half miles northeast of Cape Henlopen and takes its name from Cornelis Jacobsen Mey, a Dutch explorer who traversed the area in 1624. The first lighthouse at Cape May was built in 1823, but, long before the demise of its Cape Henlopen counterpart, it, too, succumbed to the

inroads of the sea. A new structure of 1847 proved to be too short to serve its navigational purpose and was replaced by another 170 feet in height, sketched here in 1890 by J. H. Moser through his hotel window. Throughout much of the nineteenth century, as to the present, the town of Cape May has been a popular summer resort frequented by tourists as prestigious as Presidents of the United States. *(S. Robert Teitelman Collection)*

4. DAVID J. KENNEDY's watercolor sketch of Cape May Point, dated 15 April 1875, captures the spirit of a late afternoon scene just as the seasons are about to turn. Ladies and gentlemen promenade on the beach, and the presence of a parasol or two suggests that the hazy, setting sun is uncommonly warm. What luck the fisherman has enjoyed is anyone's guess, as is also the destination of the steamer clearing the Capes – Liverpool, perhaps. The two-masted schooner lying

3

5

offshore could be from anywhere, yet it is tempting to speculate that she has carried a cargo of ice from Maine to Philadelphia in anticipation of muggy weather to come. *(Historical Society of Pennsylvania)*

5. DAVID J. KENNEDY was a prolific, talented artist whose watercolor brush recorded for posterity scenes not easily captured during the infancy of photographic technology. His 1852 view of the Cape May steamboat landing anticipates more modern scenes of the passenger and motor vehicle ferries that still cross the mouth of Delaware Bay. Here, passengers board the side-wheeler *Delaware,* which that year joined the steamers *Penobscot* and *Kennebec* on a daily run between Philadelphia and New York City, calling at Cape May en route. The *Delaware* was 219 feet in length and sported a cabin on deck. Her walking beam eleven-foot stroke piston propulsion mechanism can be seen just aft of the funnel. She ended her commercial service in 1861 for military application during the Civil War and was lost by running aground inside St. John's Bar, Florida, during the month of May 1864. *(Historical Society of Pennsylvania)*

6. INSIDE THE BAY, beyond Cape Henlopen, lies the old pilot town of Lewes, Delaware, from which artist Augustus Kollner on 5 August 1841 illustrated an Eagle Hotel patron, spyglass in hand, about to take a closer look at the shipping riding to anchor within the Delaware Bay breakwater. Surveys for the breakwater, approximately 100 miles downriver from Philadelphia, commenced about 1825 in an effort to provide safer waters for vessels entering and leaving Delaware Bay. They culminated over the years in the construction of a man-made harbor built of stone quarried along the Brandywine River above Wilmington, Delaware. By 1895, the breakwater was half a mile long and rose twelve feet above the surface of the Bay from a depth of twelve to twenty feet. During the days of sail, vessels proceeding upriver or down were at the mercy of the elements, and the breakwater became a coveted stopping-place along the Middle Atlantic coast. (*Delaware Art Museum: Samuel and Mary R. Bancroft Collection*)

Lewistown, Delaw.   August. 5. 1841.   Breakwater, Delaware Bay.

7. THE FIRST STONE of the Delaware Bay breakwater was sunk during the year 1828, and in 1848 a lighthouse was built at one end. George Emerick Essig, a pupil of marine artist Edward Moran, painted this lively watercolor of the scene in 1881. By that time, a consortium of Delaware Valley shipping interests had formed the Philadelphia Maritime Exchange to promote "the acquisition, preservation and dissemination of maritime and other business information," in order to encourage regional commerce. Essig's painting not only depicts a pilot schooner, at the far left, beating into the Bay and such mundane objects as privies precariously perched over the edge of the breakwater but also the Exchange's reporting station alongside the lighthouse. From here, news of arriving and departing vessels was signaled upriver to the shipping merchants of New Castle, Wilmington, and Philadelphia. *(Philadelphia Maritime Museum: Loan from the J. Welles Henderson Collection)*

8. A DETAIL from an undated lithograph by Thomas S. Dando provides an encompassing aerial view of the entrance to Delaware Bay as it appeared during the 1880's. Cape Henlopen Light (lower left) mirrors the Cape May Light (upper right), both of which were visible at sea from eighteen nautical miles. On the 2,550-foot southerly breakwater are situated the fixed beacon light, the Maritime Exchange signal station, a fog bell audible six miles away, and the Western Union and Anglo-American Cable office telegraph lines. These wires ran along the breakwater, dove underwater to the Cape Henlopen beacon and then snaked overland to Philadelphia. The more northerly breakwater, 1,360 feet in length, served as a barrier against ice. The gapway between the two was filled in during the early 1890's, and, by the end of the century, a second breakwater, two-and-a-quarter miles north of the first, was completed to provide the only harbor of refuge between Sandy Hook, New Jersey, and the entrance to Chesapeake Bay. An ice-proof Iron Pier, screwed into the Bay bottom and 1,700 feet long, is seen at the middle left. *(Free Library of Philadelphia)*

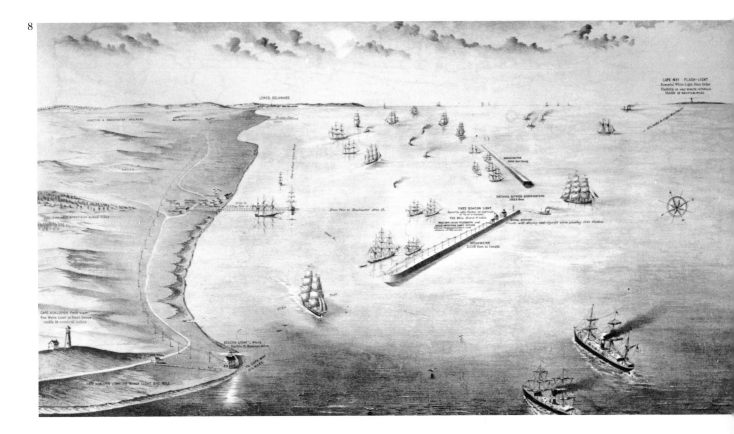

10

9. As observed from the Iron Pier, the steam tug *International* plows through cakes of drift ice in the breakwater harbor on 26 January 1893. *(Atwater Kent Museum)*

10. Following a storm of "unprecedented severity" in February 1899, more than a dozen coasting schooners lie immobilized in harbor or against the Iron Pier awaiting the arrival of an icebreaker and a tow upriver. The Maritime Exchange signal station is just barely visible against the horizon. *(Philadelphia Maritime Museum)*

11. *City Ice Boat No. 2* was launched in 1868, rebuilt and equipped in 1902 with two oil-burning 1,000 HP engines, and retired after the severe winter of 1948, during which she helped to keep a channel open through the ice between Philadelphia and Trenton, New Jersey. Owned by the City of Philadelphia, she was one of the three ice boats in operation on the Delaware River at the turn of the century. All were vital ingredients in keeping the waterway navigable throughout the year. *(Philadelphia Maritime Museum)*

12. GEORGE EMERICK ESSIG painted a view of *City Ice Boat No. 3* towing a partially dismasted vessel upriver in 1877. *City Ice Boat No. 1* was built in 1837 by Van Dusen and Birely and

was the world's first steam-powered icebreaker. Her original engine was built by Philadelphia's Matthias W. Baldwin, who later won fame for the manufacture of railroad locomotives. *No. 1* worked the river for over eighty years. The last addition to the fleet, the *John Weaver,* was launched from the Cramp shipyard in Philadelphia on 23 December 1905. She replaced *No. 3,* built in 1873 and lost during the night of 5 February 1905 when she drifted onto a wreck in the harbor of refuge and sank. The *John Weaver* was finally idled in 1940 and sent to the breaker's yard in 1952. *(Philadelphia Maritime Museum)*

LIGHTHOUSE AND MARITIME EXCHANGE REPORTING STATION, BREAKWATER

MARITIME EXCHANGE REPORTING STATION AT NEW CASTLE

13. THE Philadelphia Maritime Exchange signal station on the breakwater was only the extremity of its vessel-watching network. Other observation points came into existence during the latter part of the nineteenth century at such places as Cape May, Lewes, the Reedy Island quarantine station, New Castle, and Marcus Hook. Information from its outer branches was relayed by telegraph to the main offices in Philadelphia. Successive modernizations introduced telephonic and radio communications. The Exchange, lodged over the years in such City landmarks as the Chamber of Commerce Building, the Merchants' Exchange, the Bourse, and the Lafayette Building continues to this day as a regional shipping communications and information center. *(Philadelphia Maritime Museum)*

15   CAPE HENLOPEN LIGHT

BRANDYWINE SHOAL LIGHT

14. BEGINNING in 1883, a branch of the United States Navy's Hydrographic Office opened in conjunction with the Exchange. It offered a wide range of complimentary services to mariners, including the comparison and correction of charts, barometers, and chronometers against standard instruments. Periodically, the office also operated a time ball three feet in diameter, mounted on a staff affixed to the roof. Precisely at noon, the ball was dropped by telegraphic signal from the U.S. Naval Observatory in Washington, thus permitting shipmasters in port to observe its fall and adjust erratic chronometers accordingly. This photograph was taken in October 1895, shortly after the Exchange and Branch Hydrographic Office

14

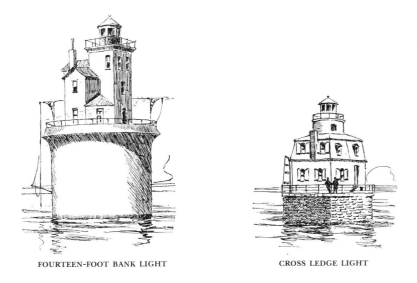

FOURTEEN-FOOT BANK LIGHT

CROSS LEDGE LIGHT

SHIP JOHN SHOAL LIGHT

relocated in the new Bourse Building on Fourth Street north of Chestnut. The seated man is probably the officer in charge at that time: Lieutenant-Commander James Russell Selfridge, USN. *(Philadelphia Maritime Museum)*

15. DURING the days of sail, vessels maneuvered up or down the Delaware River only as favoring breezes and tidal currents allowed. Even then, pilots and shipmasters had to be forever on guard against shifting shoals, shelving water, fluky winds and other natural dangers. As the nineteenth century progressed, antiquated aids to navigation haphazardly placed or maintained in earlier days were replaced with more permanent buoys, beacons, or lightships. At the end of the century, exclusive of range lights built on both the Delaware and New Jersey shores, four lighthouses rose out of the Bay between the Capes and Bombay Hook. The light on Brandywine Shoal, shown here with the other three, was built in 1850, replaced in 1913-1914, and became the last manned beacon in the Delaware. On 15 September 1974, its keepers abandoned it to electronic automation. *(Philadelphia Maritime Museum)*

16. THROUGHOUT HISTORY, port cities have been especially susceptible to the introduction of infectious diseases such as smallpox, cholera, and yellow fever. Philadelphia, which formerly disembarked huge numbers of foreign immigrants, has been no exception. A virulent outbreak of yellow fever in 1797 led to the construction of a quarantine facility, known as the "Lazaretto," at Tinicum, near Essington and Darby Creek, just

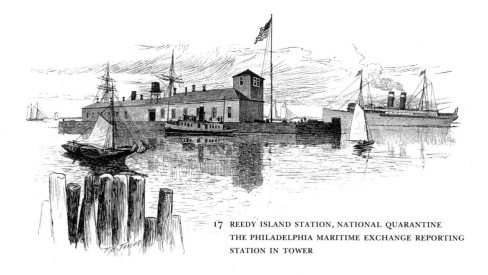

below the present-day Philadelphia International Airport. Shown here in a nineteenth-century watercolor by James Queen, which includes the bonus of market gunners hunting rail birds in its surrounding marshes, the Lazaretto and its outbuildings could accommodate as many as 500 infected patients. Lazaretto doctors inspected incoming ships and quarantined those persons aboard who were suspected of harboring pestilential disorders. *(Private Collection)*

17. ON 1 August 1884, the federal government opened another quarantine facility near the Iron Pier between Cape Henlopen and Lewes, which until 1893 worked in conjunction with the Philadelphia-operated Lazaretto by examining vessels arriving from infected ports or reporting disease on board. All others proceeded directly to Tinicum. A cholera scare in 1892, however, proved that the national quarantine station opposite the breakwater could not handle the workload quickly enough. Therefore, in 1893, another national

17 REEDY ISLAND STATION, NATIONAL QUARANTINE
THE PHILADELPHIA MARITIME EXCHANGE REPORTING
STATION IN TOWER

disinfecting station, illustrated here, came into being at Reedy Island, and the Lazaretto's administration was taken over by the State. In 1895, the facility was relocated at Marcus Hook, where, by 1913, federal and state quarantine operations had been merged. *(Philadelphia Maritime Museum)*

18. SINCE 1896, Delaware River pilots have been organized as the "Pilots' Association for the Bay & River Delaware." In earlier times, pilots owed no allegiance to anyone but themselves. Their boats were their personal property or were owned in common with small cadres of shareholders. Rivalry was keen; the first boat to reach a ship collected the fee. All that had changed by the end of the nineteenth century, however, save for a healthy competitive spirit between Pennsylvania pilots and their Delaware peers. Here, undergoing repairs or maintenence, is the Delaware pilot schooner *E. W. Tunnell* of Lewes, built at Brooklyn, N.Y., in 1887 by C. & R. Poillon and in service on the Delaware River until 1896. *(Peabody Museum of Salem, Massachusetts)*

19. THE *E. W. Tunnell*'s Pennsylvania counterpart was the schooner *William W. Ker*. A new vessel in 1890, she temporarily

8   19

survived the formation of the Pilots' Association in December 1896 and the construction of its first steam-powered pilot vessel, the *Philadelphia*. The last of the working Delaware River pilot schooners, the *J. Henry Edmunds*, ended her days in 1928 after running aground during a fog. *(Peabody Museum of Salem, Massachusetts)*

20-22. SERVICE CRAFT have had a traditional role in the workings of the river, not the least of which are the tugs that tow, push, or shove less mobile floating objects from place to place. Towing craft came early to the Delaware River following the perfection of steam propulsion and remain very much a part of it today despite formative changes in vessel design, propulsion systems, and fuel. David J. Kennedy's sketch of the 1839 freight side-wheel towboat *Lehigh (Historical Society of Pennsylvania)* contrasts starkly with a photograph, dating from about the time of World War I, showing the tugs *Maurice* (built 1892), *Neptune* (1885), and *Helen* (1901) sitting high and dry in a floating drydock, believed to have been in the Kensington section of the City. The occasion which prompted their crews to "dress ship" is unknown. More modern Curtis Bay and Independent Pier tugs, including the latter's *Triton*, surround the Bristol City Line (Canada) Ltd. passenger/cargo ship *Gloucester City* in the late 1950's or early 1960's. *(Philadelphia Maritime Museum)*

23

24

23. FIREBOATS may not turn corners on their side wheels or send horses into a frenzy or drive motorists onto the sidewalk, but they are just as important as their land-based counterparts, and sometimes they are more impressive. They are crucial adjuncts to any port's damage control capabilities. The *Edwin S. Stuart,* pictured here at the Race Street Wharf, was Philadelphia's first fireboat. Built in Brooklyn, New York, she was ordered in October 1892 for $9,800. Her mustachioed crew makes a smart appearance as it poses for a City photographer in 1908. The idlers atop the pier seem to be more numerous than gawkers at a construction site. *(City Archives of Philadelphia)*

24. THE *Bernard Samuel* has been a fixture around Philadelphia since she was built in Camden, New Jersey, in 1948. The port's modern fireboats are diesel-powered and can pump 1,500 gallons a minute with each of their four centrifugal pumps. They perform rescue missions, tow disabled vessels, fight fires aboard ships, supply water for ground forces, and, as shown in this photograph of 1980, occasionally show off. The *Bernard Samuel* and her sisters are often official "greeters" of special vessels arriving in Philadelphia. *(Philadelphia Maritime Museum)*

25. WITHOUT such specialized vessels as the U.S. Army Corps of Engineers' dredge *Comber,* few commercial or naval ships could wend their way upriver as far as Philadelphia, let alone traverse the remaining twenty-eight nautical miles to the head of navigation at Trenton, New Jersey. Some eight million cubic yards of underwater material, it has been estimated, have been removed annually during recent years from the Delaware estuary by government and private dredging companies. The *Comber,* 351 feet in length and built in 1947, dredged the lower reach from Philadelphia to the sea until her retirement in the early 1980's. Known as a "hopper" dredge, she employed drag-arm pipes 108 feet long and thirty inches in diameter to vacuum bottom effluvia into six midship hoppers holding 3,710 cubic yards of debris which was discharged later at a disposal area. When cutting a swath along the river bed, the *Comber* cruised at approximately three knots, removing some 13,000 cubic yards every day, twenty-four hours a day, seven days a week. *(Philadelphia Maritime Museum)*

25

26

26. AMONG the more important places along the banks of the Delaware River is New Castle, Delaware. Situated approximately thirty miles closer to the Atlantic Ocean than Philadelphia, it became an early port of entry for ships coming upriver from the sea and developed a strong saltwater economy as an outfitter of ships, way-station for sailing and steam packets, exporter of flour, and haven for shad and sturgeon fishermen. Frequently free of ice when freshwater Philadelphia was not, New Castle was a notable point of winter embarkation. The town was the county seat until 1881. Ives Le Blanc captured its

charming appearance on Independence Day 1797. *(Rockwood Museum: Private Collection Loan)*

27. A FEW MILES upstream of New Castle lies Wilmington, the seat of New Castle county, and now the largest city in the state of Delaware. Gracefully seated on the banks of the Christina and Brandywine Rivers, Wilmington thrived as a port from early days and became a leader in industry and ship-building. In 1802, E. I. du Pont began manufacturing gun-

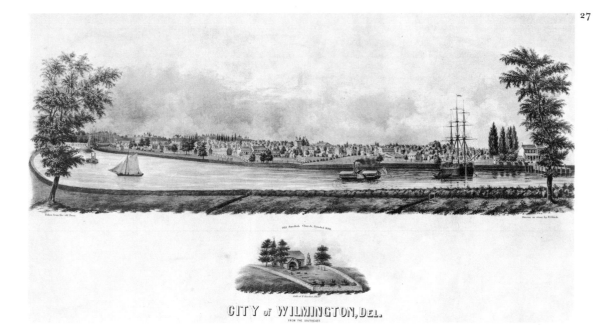

CITY of WILMINGTON, DEL.

powder in his mills along the Brandywine, establishing an industrial empire that, in more modern guises, continues to this day as a pervasive factor of the city's well-being. Today, Wilmington has joined with other Delaware River ports as one of the "Ports of Philadelphia." It is viewed here as it appeared about 1841 in a lithograph of B. Gluck/T. Sinclair. *(New York Public Library: Astor, Lenox and Tilden Foundations, I. N. Stokes Collection)*

28. ON the western side of the river between Wilmington, Delaware, and Chester, Pennsylvania, lies Marcus Hook, a sprawling oil terminal and refinery area. That the processing of petroleum became one of the region's economic bonanzas should come as no surprise when it is recalled that it was at Oil Creek, near Titusville, Pennsylvania, where, in 1859, Edwin

Drake made the world's first commercially viable oil strike. The photograph shows the Sun Oil Company's Marcus Hook barrel house and pier during World War I, when Allied vessels were taking on oil to fuel the European war effort. Sun Oil received its first delivery of crude at its new Marcus Hook facility on 20 March 1902 from the S.S. *Paraguay*. A former Great Lakes ore carrier, the *Paraguay* had been converted by the Sun Oil Company into an 18,000-barrel tankship. A few years later, she was cut in half and lengthened fifty feet, which increased her capacity by sixty-seven percent. *(Philadelphia Maritime Museum)*

29

29. A SHIP sailing or steaming up to Philadelphia must make many precision changes in course to stay within the dredged channel. The pilot accomplishes this feat by following specific reference marks such as buoys within the stream and range lights visible from it. Thus, the twenty-five mile run from Wilmington to Philadelphia, for example, requires accurate transit of eleven segments (ranges) on the river: Cherry Island, Bellevue, Marcus Hook, Chester, Eddystone, Little

Tinicum, Billingsport, Mifflin, Eagle Point, Horseshoe Bend, and Horseshoe. David J. Kennedy's watercolor of July 1864 illustrates an old range mark removed in 1881, a blockhouse light opposite historic Fort Mifflin. (*Historical Society of Pennsylvania*)

30. SEVERAL YEARS before the outbreak of the American Revolution the Province of Pennsylvania, using British plans, began construction of a fort on Mud Island later to be known as Fort Mifflin. Located at the confluence of the Delaware and Schuylkill Rivers, a few miles downriver from central Philadelphia, Mud Island has since been assimilated by the mainland and forms the northeastern boundary of today's Philadelphia International Airport. What the British stonemasons left unfinished, the Americans completed with stakes, debris, and tons of earth, enabling them for more than a month during the autumn of 1777 to distract from other predatory adventures the invading forces of General Sir William Howe and his brother Vice Admiral Richard Lord Howe. During the siege, Fort Mifflin was leveled. It is shown here in a 1960 photograph by James L. Dillon as rebuilt in the late 1790's by the administration of John Adams. (*Philadelphia Maritime Museum*)

31. AFTER passing Fort Mifflin, one of the first nineteenth-century landmarks to herald a river traveler's approach to Philadelphia was the twin ship houses of the United States Navy Yard at Wharton Street in the Southwark district. English-born artist Thomas Birch, who emigrated to the Philadelphia area with his artist father William in 1794, frequently included the buildings in his oil paintings of the harbor. In Thomas's painting of about 1840, they loom large against the shore behind the sleek topsail schooner with raked masts. Beyond the ship houses, and to their left, rises Sparks' shot tower, while the multi-decked warship moored to their right is probably meant to be the U.S.S. *Pennsylvania,* launched from the Yard in 1837. A comparative study in motive power is provided by the rowers aboard the sloop and rowboat, the ship-rigged vessel coming down behind them, and the paddle steamer headed for the Chestnut Street Wharf. She is the 279-ton *Robert Morris,* built in 1830 by John Vaughan of the city's Kensington section for the Citizens' Union Line. At one time, the *Robert Morris* departed Philadelphia at 8 AM each Monday, Wednesday, and Friday for a 4 PM disembarkation of passengers at Cape May and returned on the same schedule the days following. *(The Library Company of Philadelphia)*

31

32. ANOTHER CANVAS by Thomas Birch, also circa 1840, brings the observer closer to the ship houses and begins to detail other features of the Philadelphia waterfront. A different side-wheeler churns down river, leaving crowded city wharves in her wake. Astern of the ship just weighing anchor and between the two pole masts of the small sailboat in the foreground rises the prominent white spire of Christ Church, erected between 1752 and 1754 atop the building of 1727. The alluvial islands in midstream are Windmill and Smith's. At the far right is Cooper's Point in Camden, New Jersey. *(The Newark Museum)*

33. TRAVELERS journeying downriver towards Philadelphia from Bristol, Trenton, or points east and north enjoyed an entirely different perspective of the city as they approached it. Archibald Robertson, an engineer in the British Army, sketched this tranquil early morning scene on Friday, 28 November 1777, only two weeks after the Americans had been forced to flee the shambles of their fort on Mud Island. The Christ Church steeple again dominates the scene (center), as it overlooks waterfront activity as well as the artist, himself, sketching under the bemused eye of a local inhabitant, his wife, and child. Robertson's vantage point is not clear, but the small bay in the foreground, cut by a thin causeway, precludes the possibility of its having been taken from the New Jersey side or from Petty's Island, both of which are half a mile distant from the Pennsylvania shore. A more likely location is near the mouth of Cohocksink Creek, which once emptied into the Delaware River near Treaty Park in Kensington. *(New York Public Library: Astor, Lenox and Tilden Foundations, Spencer Collection)*

34. ADDITIONAL EVIDENCE that Robertson's view was sketched from Kensington is derived from an identifiable scene painted nineteen years later, in 1796, by John James Barralet. The placement and relative angles between the spires of Christ Church and of what probably is the tower of

33

34

the Second Presbyterian Church are virtually identical. Here, the artist depicted the ancient elm tree of Shackamaxon, later Kensington, under which, according to legend, William Penn concluded his treaty with the Indians in November 1682. While two goats eye each other from the tree branches, workmen on the pier have used a wharf-head capstan to heave a vessel down for breaming: burning old tar and tallow off the hull. A hitch of horses drags a spar from the wharf using a timber wheel. Raw spars have been stored in the water to prevent drying out before use in the shipyard at left, where the stem of a new vessel presages a launching in weeks to come. The excursionists stepping ashore from their wherry are too late; a stagecoach has already rumbled past headed for central Philadelphia. The old elm blew down during the night of 5-6 March 1810 and has since been memorialized by a monument at the foot of Columbia Avenue. *(Private Collection: Philadelphia Maritime Museum Photograph)*

35. A LATE-EIGHTEENTH-CENTURY downriver voyager would have had immense difficulty recognizing Philadelphia's waterfront a hundred years later. A. Staehle's 1881 oil painting of the harbor clearly demonstrates the development that had taken place during the time. The city's humming industrial complex was earning it the nickname of "Workshop of the World." The Christ Church steeple, while still visible, had become much less so than before; sailing ships continued to crowd the port, but steam colliers, freighters, tugs, and ferryboats were increasingly evident at every turn. The perspective chosen by Staehle is from north to south. Bearing in mind that Philadelphia numbers its piers in ascending order north or south from the perpendicular of Market Street, the dividing line in this view lies approximately to the left of center.

35

Sparks' shot tower reappears above and to the left of the little sloop's gaff. The ship houses are no longer in evidence as the Navy Yard had been removed from Southwark to League Island at the mouth of the Schuylkill River. *(Philadelphia Maritime Museum: Loan from the J. Welles Henderson Collection)*

36. ALTHOUGH William Penn's original Delaware River to Schuylkill River grid plan for his "greate towne" had blossomed luxuriantly, this bird's-eye lithographic view of Philadelphia, circa 1850, shows that the city had not yet sprawled significantly upriver beyond the Northern Liberties or downstream past Southwark. Christ Church steeple, usually gleaming white against the sky, is here depicted black against the buildings surrounding it. To its left, High Street, now known popularly as Market Street, bisects the city from river to river. Covered stalls, in which local farmers sold meat and produce until the last of the sheds was demolished about 1860, march westward up the center of the street. A ferry slip at the foot of Market Street connects with Camden, New Jersey, on the opposite side of the Delaware, as do others elsewhere along the river's edge. At the very center of the picture may be seen the rounded portico of the Merchants' Exchange, and at the left, near the old Navy Yard, Sparks' shot tower belches smoke like a factory chimney. *(Philadelphia Maritime Museum: Loan from the J. Welles Henderson Collection)*

37. BY THE YEAR 1910, when an unknown but intrepid aerialist took this picture, Philadelphia had spread unchecked almost to the limit of his low-altitude horizon. The photographer's line of sight was directly into the city's industrial heart, the Great Northeast, where spewing smokestacks and fiery furnaces converted raw materials shipped in by rail or water into modern machines and consumables sent right back into the marketplace. In the foreground lies the Market Street ferry terminal. One ferry is about to conclude its run from the New Jersey side as another prepares to leave. At the height of the ferry business some fifteen years later, 100,000 passengers were serviced daily at ten cents a ride. During peak periods, there was a departure from each side of the river every three

37

minutes. Flanking the slip are old-fashioned single-story pier buildings with shed roofs, destined soon to be replaced with structures of more modern construction. *(City Archives of Philadelphia)*

38. VIEWED AGAIN in 1929, but from an opposing direction, the Market Street ferry (bottom, center) has itself undergone modernization, and its neighboring piers have been rebuilt. However, the dominant feature in this photograph is the new Delaware River Bridge, now called the Benjamin Franklin Bridge, which, at the time of its completion, was a marvel of engineering and the longest suspension bridge in the world. In length 1.81 miles, the bridge was begun on 6 January 1922 and finally opened to the public over four years later, on 1 July 1926. Beyond the bridge, on the New Jersey side, is Cooper's Point with its radial pier configuration of rail terminals, dry docks, and berthing facilities. At the upper right is Petty's Island; at the upper left is the Delaware generating station of the Philadelphia Electric Company, sandwiched between Penn Treaty Park below and the then disused shipyards of William Cramp & Sons a short distance above. It is interesting to note that not one sailing vessel can be discerned in this picture. *(City Archives of Philadelphia)*

38

39. A SWEEPING aerial view of Philadelphia in 1928 clearly shows not only its continuing urban spread and the upward physical growth of the Center City area but also the vitality enjoyed by the region in pre-Depression days. In the foreground is New Jersey below downtown Camden and the slipways of the New York Shipbuilding Company. Directly opposite are new piers which had been constructed within the past decade upon Greenwich Point, known as the Moyamensing Group. At the far left, with the double shed, is Pier 98 South: the Philadelphia Tidewater Terminal. Next but two upriver, with the multi-level white warehouse, Pier 84 South had recently been completed through the joint ventures of the Baltimore & Ohio Railroad and the Reading Railroad, as a terminal for perishables. The B & O's foreign and coastwise terminals were located above at Pier 78 South. Not all the freighters in the river are in motion; most of them are anchored in the Greenwich Point Anchorage. *(City Archives of Philadelphia)*

40. A SIMILAR VIEW was photographed in 1984. The vantage point is from mid-river and somewhat more southerly than the previous one. The nearest bridge is the Walt Whitman, opened on 16 May 1957; the huge terminal facility in the foreground is the Packer Avenue Marine Terminal, operated by the Lavino Shipping Company. Here modern roll-on/roll-off and container handling equipment speeds the loading and unloading of ships in port. The double-shed Pier 98 South reappears on the far side of the bridge. Beyond it is the Philadelphia Electric Company's Southwark generating station. A keen eye may discern a tall white chimney rising farther alongshore against the vehicular ribbon of Route I-95. Just beyond once stood the twin ship houses of the old Navy Yard. The burgeoning Penn's Landing development project is barely visible on the downriver side of the Benjamin Franklin Bridge. Camden, New Jersey, projects into the river at the upper right. *(Philadelphia Port Corporation: Stephenson Air Photos)*

41-44. CARGO handling methods have been revolutionized during the twentieth century and have had much to do with the success or failure of port cities. The four accompanying illustrations demonstrate several of the stages through which Philadelphia cargo handling procedures have passed during the last 100 years. A longshoreman unloads raw fertilizer into a horse drawn tip cart for the Baugh Chemical Company, a dealer in superphosphates, during the late 1890's. The scoop is hand operated, rigged to the main yard of the delivering square-rigger. Conventional motorized, movable cranes deliver bags and boxes of piecemeal cargo to the nuclear-powered ship *Savannah* during the 1960's. The League Island Navy Yard's gigantic hammerhead crane, with a capacity of 350 tons at a 115-foot radius, places a 264-ton reactor aboard the Holland-American Line ship *Kamperdyk* in May 1963. Installed by such Philadelphia terminals as Packer and Tioga during the late 1970's, German-made Kocks cranes ease the handling of cargo containers and other objects of even greater weight. *(Philadelphia Maritime Museum)*

41

42

43

44

45. THE RESPONSIBILITY of day-to-day people handling on the Delaware River fell largely on the ferries, and, before the construction of multiple bridges across the more modest Schuylkill River, the same held true for that stream as well. Following settlement of the region, the first ferries were little more than small boats rowed, paddled, or poled from one shore to another. One such was illustrated by David J. Kennedy in a watercolor copied from an earlier conceptual work by Thomas Birch. It represents a Philadelphia-Camden ferry of about 1779 approaching Joseph Cooper's tavern and ferry house on Cooper's Point. The boat is double-ended with steering sweeps at each extremity. Two men row "forward," while another steers from "aft." Four passengers chat together, leaving a fifth to calm the team hitched to their coach. Hauled up on shore are two other boats, ready in reserve for moments when business was brisk. More mechanized conveyances, such as "team-boats" employing horse-treadle power, came into being in later years; nonetheless, all major crossings were serviced by steam propulsion well before the middle of the nineteenth century. *(Camden County Historical Society)*

46. A LATE-NINETEENTH-CENTURY ferry, depicted by George Emerick Essig, contends with ice floes during a mid-winter crossing. Frequently acting as their own icebreakers,

steam ferries coped valiantly with the elements and only rarely were totally stopped. The last time the Delaware River at Philadelphia froze thick enough to bring all traffic to a protracted halt was in 1895; even so, ice eighteen-inches thick was reported in parts of the river as recently as January 1985. *(The Mariner's Museum of Newport News, Virginia)*

47. TYPICAL of the twentieth-century ferries joining Philadelphia to Camden or Gloucester, New Jersey, was the Reading Railroad System's *Atlantic City.* Like her ancestral prototypes, she was also double-ended and equipped with two pilot houses to obviate the need for turning around after clearing a slip. She is shown here in October 1936 with an amphibian airplane that had just inaugurated a thrice-daily, fifty-minute flight between the foot of Bainbridge Street and the East River of New York City at Thirty-Third Street. *(City Archives of Philadelphia)*

48. IT MIGHT be supposed that the opening of the Benjamin Franklin Bridge in midsummer 1926 would have ended all local ferry service across the Delaware within a few short months or, at most, a year. Surprisingly, the final ferry run between Camden and Philadelphia was not made until the

end of March 1952. The *Haddonfield* had that distinction and is shown here earlier with the *Haddon Heights*. (*Atwater Kent Museum*)

49. THE City of Brotherly Love, unlike many other prominent port cities, has at present no one single waterfront wonder which, when pictured to the outside world, instantly says "Philadelphia!" Nowadays, there are a dozen or more suspension bridges in the United States even longer than the Benjamin Franklin Bridge. London has its picturesque Tower Bridge and Westminster Bridge with Big Ben overlording one end of it; Manhattan touts its stolid Brooklyn Bridge and the

Statue of Liberty in her flowing robes; San Francisco Bay revels in the oft cloud-covered harp-like Golden Gate Bridge. Philadelphia, in contrast, lacks an instantly recognizable maritime feature. The city has always been viewed to best advantage from Camden, yet, even though the scene is formidable, it is not spectacular. The omnipresent City Hall tower, topped by Alexander Milne Calder's thirty-seven-foot statue of William Penn, comes close to establishing an urban identity from the river side. But, as developers agitate to construct skyscrapers higher than the crown of Billy Penn's hat, even that, too, may vanish from sight. In 1843, Augustus Kollner sketched a wharfhead daydreamer near Cooper's Point in Camden, contemplating Philadelphia's watery side. *(Museum of Fine Arts, Boston: M. & M. Karolik Collection)*

Delaware River Coopers Point, Pettys Isl.d Philad.a

50. PERHAPS Augustus Kollner enjoyed the ferry ride, but, for whatever the reasons, his artistic perambulations kept taking him back to Camden, where he sketched the town as it looked in 1854. Windmill and Smith's Islands are delineated in midstream but without any indication of the baths and beer gardens that had propelled the latter into the annual fair-weather recreational outings of Camden residents and Philadelphians alike. The Market Street ferry slip is much in evidence at the end of the wide boulevard: another ferry landing at the foot of Federal Street is less so but may be discerned as the square "gallows" under Windmill Island. Philadelphia, across the river, is engulfed by an artistic mist as if it did not exist. *(Free Library of Philadelphia)*

51. KOLLNER's derivative lithograph of 1856, however, makes up for the omission and depicts the Philadelphia skyline in considerable detail. *(S. Robert Teitelman Collection)*

52. COOPER'S POINT, on the northerly side of central Camden, was probably the New Jersey landing site for the first ferry to cross the river, and the Cooper family, from whom the point took its name, was intimately connected with such operations at least from the last years of the seventeenth century. By the 1730's, the Coopers appear to have had control of all the local New Jersey river ferries save those farther downriver at Gloucester, and their involvement in the business, if not always monopolistic, continued over numerous generations. Anything requiring transport used the boats, including horses, cattle, sheep, hogs, and poultry being sent to market in Philadelphia by the West Jersey farmers. Before steam and the motive power it provided, winter service was, perforce, erratic or non-existent, and regular night runs at any time of year were not successfully operated until 1842. Joseph Cooper's tavern and ferry house, painted by Augustus Kollner in 1880, must have catered to many a cold, weary, and stranded traveler during its formative days. *(S. Robert Teitelman Collection)*

53. DAVID J. KENNEDY'S watercolor of 1864 shows Cooper's Point as it then appeared from the easterly end of Smith's Island. A double-ended ferry of the period makes for the slip and a quick turnaround back to Philadelphia. Attempts to use steam ferries on the river were made as early as 1812, but more time had to pass before they became reliable, profitable, or regularly scheduled. By 1828, however, there were a dozen of them in operation between Camden and Philadelphia. Companies of shareholders began to form, replacing individual entrepreneurs by attempting to cash in on an increasingly lucrative business. Were it possible to sketch this site from the same vantage point today, the Benjamin Franklin Bridge's easterly pylons would fill much of the field of vision. *(Historical Society of Pennsylvania)*

54. ON 20 June 1864, David J. Kennedy also sketched the West Jersey Ferry, familiarly called the "Market Street Ferry," in Camden. Established about 1800, it connected Market Street, Camden, and Market Street, Philadelphia, and was one of three or four ferry companies working the waterfront. Several nineteenth-century schemes to span part or all of the river with a bridge came to naught. *(Historical Society of Pennsylvania)*

54

55. ABOUT 1893, thirty years after Kennedy's rendering, the terminal had as a next-door neighbor a small warehouse operated by the giant Knickerbocker Ice Company, which also maintained larger depots on the Delaware and Schuylkill River shores of Philadelphia as well as a Philadelphia factory that produced many of the ice wagons used on the East Coast. In the days before widespread use of mechanical refrigeration, huge crystal blocks of ice, hauled to the region from the Kennebec River of Maine, enjoyed brisk summer sales. *(Camden County Historical Society)*

55

56-57. THE PHILADELPHIAS as viewed from Camden in an oil painting of about 1830, by an unknown artist, and in a photograph taken on Thanksgiving morning of 1984 are about as similar as caviar and sturgeon. One is the product of the other, but they neither look alike nor possess the same flavor. The early twentieth-century bark *Moshulu* is one of the modern waterfront's nostalgic attractions. *(S. Robert Teitelman Collection; Photograph: The Author)*

56

57

58. PERHAPS no view of the Philadelphia waterfront, old or new, has been more widely published, more frequently circulated, and, therefore, more readily recognized than William Birch & Son's engraving of the Arch Street Ferry. Published in 1800, it was one of twenty-seven tableaux representing the City at a time when it had just ceased to be the nation's capital but was still at an apex of its political and maritime influence. Arch Street parallels Market Street and is the first principal thoroughfare above it on the north. Piers were not numbered in those days, but, if they had been, the Arch Street Ferry would have been between the inshore ends of Piers 3 and 5 North. Here was the western terminus of Cooper's Point Ferry; nearby was a wharf and warehouse belonging to Stephen Girard, Philadelphia's merchant-shipowner extradordinary; to these docks came ornate, high-pooped sailing vessels from marketplaces around the world. The ferry was approached through a small alley from Water Street, now usurped in this vicinity by Delaware Avenue. On the side of the ferry building a carved sign of a rowing boatman was affixed overhead, a bell mounted in gallows on the roof attracted the attention of the ferryman, and old cannon served as bollards to which small vessels in the dock could be made fast. *(Philadelphia Maritime Museum)*

59. TYPICAL of the ships that used the Arch Street Ferry landing and its neighboring wharves was the ship *Pigou*, built at Philadelphia in 1792. Named in honor of the head of the British East India Company's trading establishment in Canton, China, the *Pigou* herself made several voyages to the Orient. One of her captains was Richard Dale, who had served under John Paul Jones during the Revolution. Here, under Captain Jacob Lewis, the ship is being attacked by the French privateer *L'Aventure* while on a passage to Mauritius in the Indian Ocean. *(J. Welles Henderson Collection)*

60. THE 157-ton snow *Tryphena* was built in New Bedford, Massachusetts, in 1793 but was sold to Philadelphia owners in 1795. An unidentified artist, probably Mediterannean, painted her portrait about 1802 when she was commanded by Captain Porter. A "snow" is a brig with a small trysail mast stepped just aft of the mainmast. It simplified the hoisting and lowering of the spanker sail. *(Peabody Museum of Salem, Massachusetts)*

59

61. BUILT in 1800 by Joseph Grice, who operated a shipyard in the Northern Liberties section of Philadelphia, for Gustavus and Hugh Calhoun, the Philadelphia ship *South Carolina* passes astern of a British frigate during one of her trading voyages. The watercolor was painted by Antoine Roux, marine painter of Marseilles, France, in 1805. *(Mystic Seaport Museum, Inc., Mystic, CT)*

62. THE Philadelphia ship *Columbian Packet,* Captain Wheaton, takes in sail as she prepares to pass the ancient fort at the entrance to the old harbor of Marseilles. Marseilles artist, Nicolas Cammillieri, painted her in 1806. The ship was built at Marshfield, Massachusetts, in 1801 but was sailing out of Philadelphia by November 1803. *(Peabody Museum of Salem, Massachusetts)*

63. The ship *Helvetius* was built in 1804 for Stephen Girard's trade with China and India. She is shown while under the command of Captain Adam Baush, circa 1810, during a voyage to the Baltic, in a painting by Danish marine artist Jacob Petersen. *(Philadelphia Maritime Museum: J. Welles Henderson Collection)*

64. The ship *Globe* of Philadelphia swings to her anchor, circa 1831, at Whampoa Reach in the Pearl River, the limit of ocean-going navigation for vessels trading with Canton, China. Owned by John Frederick Lewis, the ship was portrayed by an unknown Chinese artist for the vessel's supercargo, Edwin M. Lewis. The painting hung for many years in the Lewis counting room in Philadelphia. *(Atwater Kent Museum)*

65

65. AMONG the more noteworthy events to have taken place at the Arch Street Ferry was the inauguration on 14 July 1790 of the world's first regularly scheduled steamboat service. Three years earlier, inventor John Fitch had successfully demonstrated to George Washington and members of the Federal (Constitutional) Convention, then meeting in Philadelphia, that harnessed steam could power a boat. His steamboat, illustrated here by a modern model, was forty-five feet in length and reached a speed of three miles per hour using side-mounted oars given a reciprocating motion by a single-cylinder, double-acting condensing engine. A subsequent steamboat, sixty feet long and equipped with an improved propulsion system, reached eight miles per hour and ran throughout the summer of 1790 between the Arch Street Ferry and Trenton, New Jersey, with intermediate stops at Burlington, Bristol, and Bordentown. Other demonstration runs were made downriver to Chester and Wilmington, but the venture was not sufficiently well patronized to be continued. *(American Philosophical Society)*

66. THE MAJOR ROADWAY linking Philadelphia's twentieth-century complex of piers is Delaware Avenue. It was not always the broad artery it is today; in fact, much of where it now lies was once well out into the Delaware River. During the time exemplified by the Birch engraving of the Arch Street Ferry, the street along the very edge of the waterfront was muddy, irregular, impeded by obstacles. and a breeding ground for disease. In 1820, Philadelphia merchant Paul Beck, Jr. proposed a plan to provide in its place a clean, wide avenue from Vine Street to Spruce Street. City officals did nothing, and the scheme was opposed by Beck's wealthy and influential rival, Stephen Girard. However, when Girard died

eleven years later he provided in his will the sum of $500,000
to improve and maintain such an avenue. Even though
Girard's plan was generally considered inferior to Beck's, the
bequest caused the creation, in 1839, of a fifty-foot-wide Delaware Avenue between Vine Street and South Street. It is pictured here, circa 1890, looking north from the junction of
Market Street a few years before it was widened again. The
ferry terminal to Camden's Federal Street shows at the right.
(Free Library of Philadelphia)

67. THE OLD FISH MARKET at the foot of Market Street was
built in 1816 to replace an earlier structure. David J. Kennedy's

watercolor of 1837 illustrates it shortly before its demolition from the northwest corner of Water Street. Behind, and out of the picture along Market Street, lay the covered sheds in which the local and New Jersey farmers offered their livestock, poultry, and produce for sale. The ferry *John Jay* appears in the background as another ferry, belching smoke behind the Fish Market, boards passengers. The slope down to the water was once steep enough here to make it an ideal place for sledding. *(Historical Society of Pennsylvania)*

68. DAVID J. KENNEDY painted this scene along the Delaware River just north of Market Street due to a personal fascination with the Say family, one of whom was a famous naturalist, western explorer, and Kennedy's uncle by marriage. Here is a Say warehouse, pressed against a tiny wooden grocery shop and separated by an alley from a block of brick stores once owned by Stephen Girard. Drying her headsails alongside Girard's Wharf is a racy-looking brig flying her owner's houseflag from the fore-masthead. Before the road was widened, masters of vessels berthed at these piers were required by the port's governing Board of Port Wardens to rig their jibbooms inboard in order for wharfside traffic to pass unimpeded. This captain, evidently, had not yet been apprised of the regulation. *(Historical Society of Pennsylvania)*

69. A SHORT DISTANCE upriver at old Pier 8 North, a typically old-fashioned mid-nineteenth-century single-story cargo shed housed a Philadelphia institution: Alexander Kerr

Bro. & Co.'s Salt Wharves. A heavily retouched photograph, circa 1880, includes the 2,208-ton, 230-foot ship *Red Cloud,* built at Quincy, Massachusetts, in 1877 for Boston owners. She was sold foreign in 1882 and, under another name, was wrecked in the Java Sea eleven years later while hauling case oil to Hong Kong. *(Free Library of Philadelphia)*

70. THE INTERIOR of a "Kensington Salt Wharf," photographed in 1899, if not in fact Kerr's establishment, is one of the few remaining pictures to show the complex mortise and tenon construction of a nineteenth-century shed-wharf roof structure. *(City Archives of Philadelphia)*

71. SIGNIFICANT CHANGES were made to Delaware Avenue, and to the configuration of the piers abutting it, between the 1890's and the 1920's. Much of the improvement was made possible by the removal from the river of Windmill and Smith's Islands, long a hazard to navigation and an obstacle for the ferries. Thus, over a two-year period beginning in October 1897, Delaware Avenue was gradually widened in the downtown area from fifty to 150 feet, and a new pier-bulkhead line was established to provide for longer and more up-to-date shipping facilities. In this photograph of 1 August 1898 workmen build the underwater foundations for a new pier to be erected at the foot of Arch Street. Behind them a wagon delivers a supply of ale to the excursion steamer *Major Reybold.* Resplendent in her pilothouse eagle, walking beam mechanism, and intricately constructed paddlebox, the *Major Reybold* had been built by Harlan & Hollingsworth of Wilmington in 1853 and continued her river service until 1907-1908. She ran between Arch Street and Salem, New Jersey, stopping en route at Chester, Pennsgrove, New Castle, and Delaware City. *(City Archives of Philadelphia)*

73

72-73. FLOATING grain elevators were once a relatively common sight in some ports. Here the *Empire,* in 1912, and the *Commonwealth,* circa 1914, rest between jobs. Such floating monstrosities give every appearance of metacentric instability; that at the slightest puff of wind or as a result of the wash of a passing tugboat they would turn turtle to do headstands on the bottom. In practice, these floating grain repositories were stable harbor platforms used to expedite the loading or unloading of grain-laden ships. Their mobility, whether self-propelled or not, was the key. Incoming or outgoing vessels did not have to await a turn for docking space adjacent, for example, to the landbased Girard Point grain elevator just inside the Schuylkill River. Instead, the floating elevators could come to them when needed. *(City Archives of Philadelphia* and *Philadelphia Maritime Museum)*

74. THE FINGER of water between the Pier 12 North freight station, on the left, and Race Street Wharf, where the three-masted schooner discharges a lumber cargo on 17 January 1900, is just about where the westerly foundation pylon of the Benjamin Franklin Bridge was constructed twenty-four years later. A healthy field of skim ice has formed on the river but does not prevent a tug from jockeying a full Baltimore & Ohio Railroad car float up against the pier. The schooner, known to

sailors as a "tern" (three masts) is the *John R. Bergen,* built by Jackson & Sharp Company of Wilmington in 1882 and owned in New York City. She had arrived on 30 December 1899 carrying lumber from Sabine Pass in the Gulf of Mexico. In early February she sailed for Savannah. *(City Archives of Philadelphia)*

75. THE BRAND-NEW four-masted schooner *Charles D. Loveland* of Bath, Maine, arrived in the Delaware River in ballast at the end of April 1916 and was photographed a month later, next to Vine Street's Pier 19 North, awaiting a cargo for Liverpool. Pier 19 had been built in 1911 as part of the program to provide Philadelphia with modern wharves capable of handling the new and larger steamers of the era. It had been equipped for all trades—foreign, intercoastal, coastwise, and river. The upper deck housed an immigration station, which ceased to be used when immigration fell off due to quotas imposed during the mid-1920's. Along Delaware Avenue a spur railroad line is being laid to shunt freights in and out of the new wharf buildings. *(City Archives of Philadelphia)*

76. AUGUSTUS KOLLNER'S 1851 watercolor of the same location, which features an array of houseboats clustered about the wharf, is in stark contrast to seventy years of "progress" in the area. *(Philadelphia Maritime Museum: Loan from the J. Welles Henderson Collection)*

75

76

78

77. UPRIVER of the Kensington section, beyond where Cohocksink Creek and the Aramingo Canal once emptied into the Delaware River, is a piece of ground identified on two-hundred-year-old maps as "Point No Point" or "Richmond." Artist Augustus Kollner painted a charming watercolor of the territory in 1847: almost virgin, idyllic, a fine place for a little fishing or hunting, and a remnant of one of Penn's original grants. *(S. Robert Teitelman Collection)*

78. ONCE coal from the interior regions of Pennsylvania began to pour into Philadelphia by rail for reshipment to the world, the unspoiled days of Point No Point came to an end. The land was bought by the Reading Railroad in 1837. By the 1850's, it was known as "*Port* Richmond." Where the waters of the Delaware had for millennia lapped against marsh grass and bullrushes, gangling coal wharves now intruded. Where autumnal hunters had once stalked game, Philadelphia & Reading Railroad Company tracks had covered the ground in a vast, fanlike network. *(Atwater Kent Collection)*

79. BY 1926, Port Richmond had a frontage of more than a mile, a sprawling terminal for anthracite and bulk items, which included iron ore from Newfoundland and the Scandinavian countries, shipped by rail to steel plants across the country. In these photographs, the steamer *Orion*, circa 1893, and a four-masted schooner load at the Reading Railroad coal piers. *(Free Library of Philadelphia)*

80. THE FIRST six-masted schooner built at the historic Percy & Small Yard in Bath, Maine, the *Eleanor A. Percy,* constructed in 1900, awaits a similar lading at a later day. *(Maine Maritime Museum)*

79

80

81. THIS PHOTOGRAPH shows a non-commercial stretch of water near the end of Allegheny Avenue in the Great Northeast, above Port Richmond. Today, the site is occupied by the massive Tioga Marine Terminal grouping. The skinny-dipper in mid-channel must either have worked nearby or have been unemployed. 15 July 1918, when the picture was taken, was a Monday, and the shadows suggest the time of day must have been around lunchtime. The craft shown are in various states of disrepair, although the motor launch *Obereta,* with awnings rigged and curtains in the window, is obviously recovering from a weekend of hard driving use. *(City Archives of Philadelphia)*

82. MANY Philadelphians took to the river in small craft during the warm weather months, some because it was a means to an income and others purely for the sport of it. Several of the boat types they used were indigenous to the Delaware River basin. Among them was the Delaware Ducker, normally about fifteen feet in length, four feet in breadth, double-ended, and lapstrake-built with a round bottom. They were also known as rail-bird boats or reed-bird skiffs and could either be rowed, sailed, or poled. The example illustrated has a "barn door" rudder. *(Mystic Seaport Museum, Inc., Mystic, CT)*

83

83. FREQUENTLY built of cedar on oak frames, Delaware Duckers were originally used by market and sport gunners in the marshy stretches along the river. A similar boat appears in the view of hunters around the Lazaretto, pictured earlier. Thomas Eakins' famous oil painting, "Starting Out After Rail," typifies these splendid little boats. *(Museum of Fine Arts, Boston: Charles Henry Hayden Fund)*

84. THOMAS EAKINS also left to posterity a bright, breezy record of another type of Delaware River small craft. His oil painting of 1874, "Sailboats Racing on the Delaware," shows a regatta of "tuck-ups" beating upwind during a Sunday afternoon race. Sixty or more at a time once could be seen racing a thirty-mile course upriver or down, depending upon the tide. First described about 1850, the tuck-up type began as a workboat for fishing, hunting, trapping, or crabbing but soon was dubbed "the working man's yacht." *(Philadelphia Museum of Art: Gift of Mrs. Thomas Eakins and Miss Mary A. Williams)*

85. THE PHOTOGRAPH shows the tuck-up *Spider,* built in 1876, sailing to victory under skipper Judson Bergman. Tuck-ups were sailed on their bottoms, not on their bilges, and required a minimum crew of four: skipper, sheet tender, ballast man, and bailer. This boat is now owned by the Philadel-

phia Maritime Museum, which uses her in conjunction with its interpretive boatbuilding programs. *(Philadelphia Maritime Museum)*

86. ANOTHER type of sailboat used on the river was the "sandbagger." Here, in a photograph by Nathaniel L. Stebbins, the Quaker City Yacht Club's *Hurley* bravely attempts to overtake two other sandbaggers forced off course by the approach of a deep-laden coasting schooner. Usually larger than either Duckers or tuck-ups, these boats carried bags of sand for ballast, which were shifted as necessary to achieve the proper trim. With a centerboard well aft, a barn door rudder, and a large area of canvas aloft, their crews had to be on their toes to prevent a capsizing. *(Society for the Preservation of New England Antiquities)*

87. FOR THOSE with larger yachts and more leisure to use them, the Corinthian Yacht Club of Philadelphia, in Essington, was the answer. Founded in 1892, the club took its

name from a term signifying an amateur yachtsman who sailed his own boat rather than hiring a professional skipper. The large steam yacht lying at anchor in the harbor, nevertheless, belies any assumption that all members polished their own brass. The vessel may possibly be the *Viking*, built in 1883 by the Delaware River Iron Shipbuilding & Engine Works at nearby Chester, Pennsylvania. In the background is Little Tinicum Island. In recent decades, the Corinthian Yacht Club's protected yacht basin has become so filled with silt it can no longer be used, obliging members to keep their boats at the New Jersey shore, in the Chesapeake, or elsewhere. *(Philadelphia Maritime Museum)*

88. PHILADELPHIANS used to get out on the wintry rivers, too, when they could. Before steam and the icebreakers came along, there were many years when the ice froze so thickly that no ships could move for as long as two or three months at a stretch. During those times, unemployment soared, jails and workhouses filled to the bursting point, and the light-at-heart went skating. A visiting Frenchman, Charles Alexandre Lesueur, sketched the icy hijinks and barbecue he witnessed on the Delaware River, in celebration of Washington's Birthday, 1825. *(American Antiquarian Society)*

89. ANOTHER mid-winter frolic on the ice in 1831, while caricaturing its participants' slippery perigrinations, suggests that such diversions helped to alleviate the February blahs. *(Atwater Kent Museum)*

90. ON 21 December 1849 "The Skaters Club of the City and County of Philadelphia," later known as "The Philadelphia Skating Club and Humane Society," was founded. Its purpose was twofold: to instruct and improve upon the art of skating and to teach the use of life-saving equipment suitable for the rescue of persons breaking through the ice. No doubt club

88

89

members were in their element during the severe winter of 1856 and are among those pictured in James Queen's souvenir lithograph, even though there are no ladders, ropes, life rings or grapnels in evidence. The merriment, including a crack-the-whip pung ride in the center, takes place in front of the old Navy Yard's ship houses. *(Philadelphia Maritime Museum: Loan from the J. Welles Henderson Collection)*

91. THE Philadelphia waterfront has also been observable from lofty, inland, vantage points. The two presented here are separated in time by almost a century and a half. The first, a print by J. C. Wild, published in 1838, is an east view of the City taken from the steeple of Independence Hall, on the southeast corner of Sixth and Chestnut Streets. Beyond the east wing is the Fifth Street pilastered facade of Library Hall, demolished in 1884 but later rebuilt. Behind it, with the end colonnade, is the Second Bank of the United States. The steeple of Christ Church rises at the upper left. *(S. Robert Teitelman Collection)*

92. THE SECOND VIEW, a photograph taken in November 1984 from atop the Public Ledger Building on the southwest corner of Sixth and Chestnut, presents a surprisingly compatible scene. One thing is common to both: the Delaware River seems far removed from daily City life. Perhaps this is one reason why Philadelphians tend to forget, and why tourists are barely aware, that the City of Brotherly Love is a port of international significance. *(Author's Photograph)*

91

92

93

93-94. TAKEN from the top of Sparks' shot tower on the north side of Carpenter Street between Second and Front Streets, these January 1870 photographs look down on the Delaware over the Queen Village section of Southwark. At the far left is the end of Windmill Island; the large building towards the right is the Washington Avenue grain elevator; and at the far right is the old Navy Yard, not yet relocated on League Island. To the left of the grain elevator, halfway between it and the coal piers, the steeple of Gloria Dei (Old Swedes') Church pierces the treetops. Between the elevator and the Navy Yard ship houses is Pier 53 South, which became one of Philadelphia's principal immigrant receiving stations. Unlike the 1929 aerial view of the river (Figure 38), in which

no sailing vessels can be seen, these photographs capture not a single steamer. (*Free Library of Philadelphia*)

95. A LANDMARK even before it opened for business on Independence Day 1808, Thomas Sparks' and John B. Bishop's shot tower has withstood the winds of time but is no longer used. Nowadays, it is a curious relic within a children's playground. For the better part of a century, however, this 140-foot high, thirty-foot diameter (base) and fifteen-foot diameter (top) brick tower produced lead shot for use in small arms, muskets, shotguns, and the like. Sparks and Bishop began as plumbers at 49 South Wharves before introducing

95

their new venture, an understandable progression when it is remembered that plumbers, by definition, were workers in lead. Molten lead was poured from the top of the tower through grids, or screens, of variable size; by the time the resulting globules reached the bottom they had become the near perfect spheres required for munitions. Bishop, a peace-loving Quaker, withdrew from the partnership during the War of 1812, when the tower's production turned from hunting purposes to wartime production. *(Author's Photograph)*

96. THE WIDENING of Delaware Avenue, which began anew in the late 1890's, was dependent upon the removal of Smith's and Windmill Islands, alluvial shoals that grew from the time of William Penn into a substantial land mass covered with willow trees. By 1746, the spit had become big enough for miller John Harding to erect a windmill on a point opposite Pine and Spruce Streets, and in 1800 three men were hanged nearby for piracy. In 1838, the deposit's natural proclivity for being two islands was artifically enhanced to create a channel for the passage of the Philadelphia-Camden ferries. The southern half garnered the name Windmill, memorializing the long-vanished structure, and the northern half became Smith's in honor of his resort. This panoramic photograph, taken by F. Gutekunst from near the foot of Chestnut Street in 1891, was taken before dredges began to obliterate the islands. In the foreground, the pleasure steamer *Twilight* rests at the end of a busy day. *(Philadelphia Maritime Museum)*

97. THE STEAMER *Twilight,* owned by the Upper Delaware River Transportation Company, was one of several steamers leaving Chestnut Street Wharf daily for Bristol, New Jersey, calling at Bridesburg, Tacony, Riverton, Torresdale, Beverly, and Burlington. At Bristol, passengers continuing on to Trenton made connections with the steamer *Trenton.* The *Twilight,* 420 tons, 176 feet long, twenty-seven feet in breadth, and 139

97

HP, was built in 1868 for Captain Henry Crawford by Harlan & Hollingsworth of Wilmington, Delaware, and ran her river route for fifty-five years. (*Philadelphia Maritime Museum*)

98-99. EXCURSIONISTS seeking the festive picnic atmosphere offered on Smith's Island boarded their ferries either at Chestnut Street Wharf or at Walnut Street Wharf, the second of which is illustrated here as it appeared about 1835.

98

99

Just to the left of the ferry slip is Bloodgood's Hotel; just to the right is the Cope Line office with two of its Philadelphia-Liverpool packets docked nearby; the towered building at the right is a seamen's Bethel church. At one time, several small steam catamarans, paddlewheels mounted between their twin hulls, shuttled every ten minutes between Walnut Street Wharf and the island, but David J. Kennedy's mid-century watercolor of Smith's Island shows rowing ferries in use. The steam ferry has nothing to do with island service; it is simply passing through the cut en route to Camden. *(Historical Society of Pennsylvania)*

100-102. THAT Smith's Island was to become a nineteenth-century workingman's watering spot derived from an enterprise which commenced soon after the War of 1812: a floating bath house was anchored at the island and opened for business during the hot, steamy months of summer. Over the course of time, the island's facilities boasted not only its bath

101   102

house and swimming facilities but also a restaurant (noted in
the spring for its planked shad), music, and beer garden.
From time to time, special events added to its popularity:
balloon ascensions, tightrope performances, and other
carnival-like attractions. From the 1880's, until the islands'
removal from the river, the baths were known as Ridgeway
Park. An advertising print illustrates some of the available
facilities *(Atwater Kent Museum)*, while stereoptican views bring
it more vividly to life. *(Private Collection)*

103. IN 1887 the Philadelphia Maritime Exchange petitioned
the United States Congress for an appropriation to study the
removal of Smith's and Windmill Islands. From a commercial
maritime standpoint, the islands not only presented an intol-
erable hazard to navigation but also prevented revision of the
Port Wardens' bulkhead line to permit the construction of
longer and more modern wharves. Two years later, the Exchange memorialized the Philadelphia City Council for funds
to acquire title to the islands. Then came a long wait. By the
end of March 1894, however, the monumental dredging operation had begun: four-and-a-half million cubic yards of
dredged material, most of which was dumped on League
Island to improve the new Navy Yard, had already been re-

moved. A total of 21,605,061 cubic yards were dredged before the project was completed in 1898. This aerial sketch of the islands was printed in *Harper's* magazine while the work was in progress. *(Philadelphia Maritime Museum)*

104. THE ISLANDS were but memories when the steamers *General Cadwalader* and *Anthony Groves, Jr.* were photographed at the northern foot of Chestnut Street shortly before Christmas 1898. Despite the season and the plumes of steam from vessels in the river, it evidently was warm enough for a man atop the aft deckhouse of the *Cadwalader* to be hosing her down in his shirtsleeves. The cold and damp along Delaware Avenue at the bottom of the winter can be an unforgettable experience. The *General Cadwalader* was an aging lady at the time, having been built at Wilmington in 1845. The *Anthony Groves, Jr.,* in contrast, was only five years out of the Charles Hillman Ship & Engine Building Company in Kensington. She made overnight runs for the Ericsson Line between Philadelphia and Baltimore via the Chesapeake and Delaware Canal. Passengers made arrangements for meals and staterooms after boarding. *(City Archives of Philadelphia)*

105. ANOTHER popular passenger boat on the river was the Wilson Line's *City of Wilmington,* launched in 1909 by Harlan &

Hollingsworth of Wilmington. She and her opposite number, the *City of Philadelphia*, hit the water fourteen minutes apart. Both were considered to be twenty years ahead of their time technologically. An advertisement of 1925 summed up what they offered the public: "Delightful Excursions On the Historic Delaware River / Morning-Afternoon-Evening / Evening Trips Carry High-Class Dance Orchestra / The Best Way to See our Great Port." It must have been a cold day on the river when this photograph was taken, though. Only two stalwarts brave the exposed upper deck, while the more sheltered accommodations below seem to be packed with humanity stowed spoon-fashion. *(City Archives of Philadelphia)*

104

105

106

106. AFTER NEW YORK CITY, Philadelphia was one of the foremost points of disembarkation in the New World for nineteenth- and early twentieth-century immigrants. Packed into steerage accommodations more overcrowded than a Delaware River excursion boat on a blustery day, they endured weeks, rather than hours, of jostling and discomfort. Once cleared through the health, immigration, and customs stations, they were on their own. The little group huddled around a lamp post at Walnut Street Wharf in David J. Kennedy's watercolor of 1851 seems, at once, to be animated and quizzical. One assumes the square-rigger behind them was their means of conveyance across the Atlantic. (*Historical Society of Pennsylvania*)

107. LATER IMMIGRANTS tended to fare better, especially after the turn of the century when steamship companies began to admit that the immigrant traffic had become their single greatest source of revenue. The American Line's steamer *Haverford*, servicing the Philadelphia-Queenstown-Liverpool route and seen here steaming down the Delaware, carried 150 second-class passengers and 1,700 third-class. Six years after she was built in 1901, the United States admitted 1,200,000 immigrants. (*Philadelphia Maritime Museum*)

108. NOT ALL passenger ships using the Delaware River realized their profits from the carriage of immigrants. The Merchants & Miners Transportation Company was established in 1852 by Baltimore and Boston backers, with the

107

intention of developing a freight business in general mer-
chandise and mine products. The company grew steadily,
adding new coastwise schedules to its repertoire, and attract-
ing passengers by providing its ships with better-than-average
accommodations. In 1900, Merchants & Miners inaugurated a
service between Philadelphia and Savannah, later extended to
include Jacksonville. Seven years afterwards, Philadelphia-
Boston service was added, and in 1925 yet another linked
Philadelphia to Miami. J. Donald Haig's retrospective oil
painting of 1966 shows the Merchants & Miners' Philadelphia
terminals at Piers 18-24 South, since obliterated to make way
for the new Penn's Landing. *(Philadelphia Maritime Museum)*

109. ENGULFED by wings of mist and water, the thirty-four-
year-old City fire-boat *Bernard Samuel* escorts the 963-foot
Cunard liner *Queen Elizabeth 2* towards Philadelphia during

her maiden transit of the Delaware River, on Sunday, 25 April 1982. The giant passenger liner/cruise ship is the last of the luxurious floating palaces that for generations ferried the famous and not-so-famous across the North Atlantic. Fast, convenient air travel ended the liner era during the 1960's. The *Queen Elizabeth 2*'s initial visit to Philadelphia commemorated the 300th anniversary year of William Penn's first arrival in Pennsylvania. Upon her return to the United Kingdom, she was requisitioned by the British government to carry troops into the Falkland Islands war against Argentina. Since then, she has returned to Philadelphia on several occasions, setting a precedent for other cruise ships to take advantage of the port's modern tourist traffic. *(Author's Photograph)*

110-111. WHEN William Penn came to inspect Philadelphia in 1682, his landing place was at the "Dock," a tidal basin connecting with the Delaware River below Spruce Street and joined by a creek flowing into it from the northwest. Their course may still be seen today in the form of Dock Street, which is totally at odds with the perpendicular street grid surrounding it, and by an otherwise bizarre depression crossing the manicured lawn

in Independence Park behind Carpenter's Hall. In the Dock Creek/Dock Street area, once a focus of Philadelphia life, many maritime enterprises lived and died. A photograph of Second Street at Dock, in 1866, pictures Irwin & Young's house- and ship-carving establishment, liberally embellished with samples of their work. Another nearby view, taken several years earlier at Dock and Water Streets, illustrates an anchor-seller's warehouse adjoining one of the countless mariners' boarding houses found in the region. Note the railroad tracks in the street and the boxcar at the far left. *(Free Library of Philadelphia)*

112. FOR A FEW YEARS just at mid-nineteenth century, another bizarre sight greeted visitors to the Dock Street Wharf: a floating church, built of wood in the best Gothic Revival architecture of the day. These were times of an increasing awareness and concern for the morals and soul of the lonely sailor: far from home, without guidance, tempted by corruption. The Floating Church of the Redeemer was the Churchmen's Missionary Association for Seamen of the Port of Philadelphia's attempt to guide Jack Tar along the straight

and narrow paths of righteousness. It was built at Borden-town, New Jersey, in 1847 by Clement L. Dennington and was moored against the Dock Street Wharf until 1851, when the pier was leased for less-godly commercial purposes. The floating church was then towed across the river to Camden, rolled over ground, and set down at the intersection of Broadway and Royden Streets. Renamed St. John's Church, it burned down one Christmas morning several years later. *(Philadelphia Maritime Museum: J. Welles Henderson Collection)*

113. MUNICIPAL PIER 16 South Delaware Wharves, photo-graphed in 1919, was one of the new piers built in 1913 as part of the city-wide program to modernize the waterfront and enable Philadelphia to compete more effectively with New York and Baltimore. Despite the newness of the building, pigeons have already made themselves at home. Although the British shipping firm of Furness, Withy & Co. Ltd. used the pier as a terminal, none of the vessels in the picture are

company vessels. On the upriver side, an unidentified naval vessel lies outboard of a Navy Yard repair barge; at the other side, a French four-masted bark from Dunkirk rides partially loaded. Pier 16, now displaced by Penn's Landing, lay at the foot of Dock and Spruce Streets, which formerly had been a depot for the South New Jersey oystermen from Maurice River and other oystering areas in the Bay. *(City Archives of Philadelphia)*

114-117. THE OYSTER BEDS on the New Jersey side of the lower Delaware River and upper Bay have for hundreds of years provided epicurean ecstacy for Philadelphians and a way of life for oystermen. Few got rich harvesting the tasty mollusks, but it was a living; the importance of the industry even gave the name "Bivalve" to a town inside the Maurice River. Great fleets of two-masted schooners–dredgeboats– once worked the beds. Then came powerboats, thinner pickings, and hard times. In the accompanying photographs, a

dredgeboat out of Leesburg, New Jersey, heaped with the day's bounty, is assisted against the tide by her pushboat. The fleet comes into the Maurice River, while the crew of the Leesburg sloop *Dottie and Burtie* tends stoically to its own affairs. The Camden dredgeboat *Admiral* sits alongside a string of floats, into which the men aboard shovel oysters off the deck to keep them fresh for market. Finally, one unidentified schooner has made quite a splash for herself that day; the gruff old-timer almost has a smile on his face, while the young man looks as pleased as punch. *(Philadelphia Maritime Museum)*

116

117

118-119. VIEWED on 8 January 1917 from a freight car opposite Pier 34 South and looking north along Delaware Avenue, old Pier 30, at the foot of Kenilworth Street, awaits the results of bidding for its turn at modernization. The photograph shows clearly the effects of widening the avenue and the newly-laid tracks, along which a switching engine moves away from the cameraman. Work on the widening of Delaware Avenue to the southward as far as Bigler Street had been completed. Almost three years later, 29 December 1919, a closer inspection reveals that form work for the pier's inshore foundations had begun. Docked at one of the Independent

118

119

Pier Company's old shed wharves is the Norwegian steel-hulled ship *Fiskjo,* taking aboard lubricating oil for shipment to Drobak and Bergen, Norway. This elegant square-rigger had been built in 1891 at Dumbarton, Scotland, under the name *Hiawatha.* The steam on deck comes from a donkey engine used to assist with loading. *(City Archives of Philadelphia)*

120-121. THE NEW Pier 30 South was completed in 1921 for the foreign trades. Proudly known at the time as one of the new Southwark Group, it joined nearby Piers 38 and 40 South, which had opened during the autumn of 1915, as a model, up-to-date ship-handling facility. It boasted concrete and steel construction, City water, electric light and power, and median interior railroad tracks capable of handling eighteen cars at a time and connecting with the Belt Line tracks in Delaware Avenue. Photographed in January 1985, Pier 30's central exterior looks much as it did sixty-four years before, but its internal use is quite different. Conversion has transformed it into a tennis pier containing eight courts. Pier 34, next door, is unused and derelict. A short distance farther down remain the vintage Piers 38 and 40 South, City-owned and still operable. The construction at the right foreshadows completion of an emergency operations center for the United States Coast Guard. *(Author's Photographs)*

122. THE SECTION of waterfront illustrated on the last several pages once catered extensively to Philadelphia's sugar refining industry. In a photograph taken during the mid-1870's, the tern schooner *A. R. Weeks* of Portland, Maine, discharges a cargo onto a sugar wharf of the Pennsylvania Sugar Refining Company, already filled to capacity. The other schooner has rigged her mizzen gaff backwards to act as a cargo boom. *(Historical Society of Pennsylvania)*

122

123. ANOTHER PHOTOGRAPH, taken in 1919, is of the Franklin Sugar Refinery's plant below Kenilworth Street. The big iron bark hails from Christiansand, Norway. To her right is the six-year-old English-built freighter *Triton*, registered in Amsterdam and owned by the Koninklijke Nederlandische Stoomboot Maatschappij. The double-paddlewheel steamboat at the left is unidentified. *(City Archives of Philadelphia)*

124. THE UPPER DECK of Pier 40 South was wall-to-wall sugar bags on 23 March 1916 – all of 8,700 tons' worth – but the weight presented no difficulties: the deck had been engineered to carry 250 pounds per square foot, and it measured 180 feet by 550 feet. In 1914, Philadelphia refined a half-million tons of raw sugar, about one-sixth of the total amount processed in the country. That year made another kind of

history: on 24 August the first vessel to reach Philadelphia via the Panama Canal steamed into the harbor. She was the American-Hawaiian Steamship Company's *Pennsylvanian*. On board were 122,835 bags of raw Hawaiian sugar consigned to the Franklin Sugar Refining Company. The American-Hawaiian Line to West Coast ports had Philadelphia sailings and arrivals every five days. (*City Archives of Philadelphia*)

125. BULKHEADING for the 900-foot Pier 78 South, at the end of McKean Street, was under way by the end of May 1916.

Over the long shed flanking the site rises Baugh's Chemical Works, a manufacturer of fertilizer since 1855. It is tempting to speculate that the large schooners nearby have hauled raw phosphates to Baugh's from Tampa or some other southern port. A few small pleasure craft in the area are a reminder that, at the time, the downriver waterfront from this point to League Island had not yet been fully built upon. *(City Archives of Philadelphia)*

126. IN THE SHALLOWS just to the north of Pier 78 there remain to this day the bones of three schooners – the *Albert D. Cummins* (built in 1920), the *Francis J. McDonald* (1917), and *Marie F. Cummins* (1920) – laid up during the Depression days, abandoned in 1933, and burned to their waterlines by order of the State Bureau of Navigation on 27 August 1947. The hulks are still visible in aerial photographs. *(Philadelphia Maritime Museum)*.

127. THE downriver waterfront above League Island was the Greenwich area, which consisted largely of low-lying, marshy ground. James Thorp Flaherty's oil painting of 1881 from Greenwich Point, looking back towards Philadelphia, confirms the slow encroachment of civilization. *(Philadelphia Maritime Museum)*

128. THE WORST BLOT on the landscape was the Pennsylvania Railroad's coal wharves and rail lines that mirrored on a smaller scale the Reading Railroad's bulk terminals at Port Richmond. On the northern fringes of this amorphous Greenwich-Moyamensing region, and not far from Baugh's

Chemical Works, Jackson Street ended in the Delaware. Here, as in other swampy waterfront locations, squatters took up residence. Their shacks must have been like tombs in winter-time. They must have reeked in the summer. The rats must have been fierce. Yet, the young women, who hold up their babies for the photographer in 1910, have coiffed and dressed themselves for him with more flair than their surroundings would suggest possible. *(Historical Society of Pennsylvania)*

129. TWO MEN below the Pennsylvania Railroad's Pier 7, Greenwich, seem less at home there in 1912 than if they had been floating through the Delaware Water Gap in the upper Delaware fifty years before. The raft of logs they attempt to

maneuver under the stern of the barge *Rose F. Hagan* is tiny in comparison with the rafts lumbermen once wrestled down-river from the hinterlands, but these men's labors seem to have been considered sufficiently archaic for the trainmen on the coal car trestle above to have stopped their own work to watch. *(City Archives of Philadelphia)*

130. IN 1864, when such sights were commonplace, David J. Kennedy sketched similar rafts hauled up along the shore next to a railroad embankment at Stewart's Point, south of Bordentown, New Jersey. *(Historical Society of Pennsylvania)*

131. NO LIVING Philadelphians in 1790 or 1825–even in 1850 or beyond–could ever, in their wildest imaginings, have pictured the transformation this beloved and tranquil river-side inn would undergo at the hands of their twentieth-century descendants. Shaded by willow trees, cooled by river breezes, away from the grime and noise of the City, the Old Point House was a favored afternoon drive and resort for the well-to-do of Philadelphia. Some boarded there for the summer, and George Washington himself was no stranger to its charming ambiance. Evidently, David J. Kennedy enjoyed it, too; his watercolor of 1846 captures an idyllic grace that modern Philadelphians would travel hundreds of miles to recapture. They don't have to. They can visit the site today simply by dodging Kocks cranes and cargo containers at the Packer Avenue Marine Terminal. *(Historical Society of Pennsylvania)*

132-134. THE OLD POINT HOUSE faced Gloucester, New Jersey, itself once unspoiled and a scene of annual springtime activity, for it was then that the shad turned up in the river to spawn. Baked shad, planked shad, shad and roe, shad roe salad: these and a host of other related dishes are traditional delicacies of the region. Thomas Eakins was among those who not only enjoyed the eating but also the painting of how the fish were netted, exemplified by his oil painting, "Shad Fishing at Gloucester on the Delaware River" *(Philadelphia Museum of Art: Gift of Mrs. Thomas Eakins and Miss Mary A. Williams)* and by his watercolor "Drawing the Seine at Timber Creek Estuary, Gloucester, New Jersey" *(John G. Johnson Collection, Philadelphia).* A photograph of the period demonstrates the enthusiasm on the beach whenever the shad were running. *(Philadelphia Maritime Museum)*

SHAD ROE SALAD

1 Lettuce	2 nice Shad Roes (cooked)
1 Lemon	Parsley

Place on a platter covered with lettuce, Shad Roe nicely trimmed and sliced in its own shape. Garnish with sliced lemon and parsley. Serve with this salad Anchovy dressing and cucumber sandwiches.

Stephen St. John Gilmore (1882-1954)
Butler, "Druim Moir"
Chestnut Hill, Philadelphia, PA

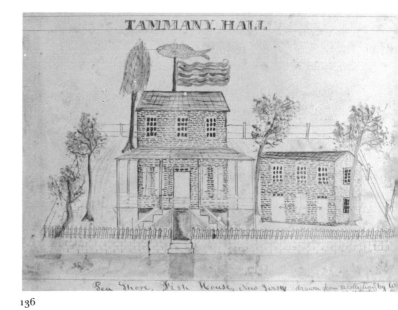

135

136

135. DAVID J. KENNEDY fortunately left behind a watercolor of one of the nineteenth-century riverside Gloucester social angling clubs, the Prospect Hill Fish House, to which he added: "Fishing by net until June 10th Shad and herring fishery." *(Historical Society of Pennsylvania)*

136. THE ANCIENT Tammany Hall Fish House, founded by Philadelphians in 1803, lay further upriver off Petty's Island, two miles or so above Camden. It was still standing in 1909. Unlike some other fishing clubs, its stockholders permitted the public to use it; some 7,000 excursionists are said to have visited it in 1850. Recollected sketch by William Rank, 24 October 1850. *(S. Robert Teitelman Collection)*

BAKED SHAD WITH ROE

2 Pounds shad	Soft bread crumbs
1 pair roe	Clarified butter
1 Tbs. chopped parsley	½ cup sauterne
Pepper, salt (if desired)	1½ cup chopped mushrooms
1 Tbs. butter	1 Tsp. paprika

Split and bone the shad. Scald the roe, split them, and scrape out the eggs, to which add the parsley, desired seasoning, butter, and a few soft bread crumbs. Stuff the shad with this mixture and secure with string. Place in baking dish and brush on clarified butter. Cook in slow (300° F) oven for 35 to 40 minutes, taking care to baste frequently with the cooking juices. Saute the mushrooms in some of these juices, add wine, heat, and pour over the shad. Garnish with lemon wedges dipped in paprika.

137. LEST it be forgotten that Philadelphia lies between *two* rivers, a sure reminder that fish have navigated the Schuylkill River, too, is The Schuylkill Fishing Company, better known as "The State in Schuylkill." Founded in 1732 as The Colony in Schuylkill, this venerable and exclusive fishing club changed its name to "State" after the American Revolution. J.E. Eastwick's painting shows its clubhouse, "The Castle," at a site near Rambo's Rock, opposite Bartram's Gardens and below Gray's Ferry on the lower stream. This was not its original location. It was moved thither in 1822, following completion of the dam at Fairmount, from its place above the dam in order for the club's "Citizens" to continue angling for such fish as shad and salmon. But in future years, the City Gas Works went into operation alongside the river, oil refineries sprang up nearby, slaughter houses dumped noisome filth into the stream, and manufacturing establishments further polluted not only the water but also the peaceful surroundings. The State in Schuylkill picked up its Castle again and moved to the Delaware River side, miles above Philadelphia. The club has occupied two sites in that region and is now a dining, rather than a fishing, society. Ironically, environmental cleanups have restored many fish to the Schuylkill. (*The State in Schuylkill*)

137

138. A 1929 AERIAL VIEW, looking southwest across the Delaware River from above Greenwich Point, pinpoints the actual confluence of the Delaware and Schuylkill Rivers beyond League Island. Little has changed over the intervening years in terms of the land mass, save for infilling of the Back Channel (seen in the foreground) to expand the League Island Navy Yard and modification of the portion beyond the causeway as a reserve basin for mothballed naval vessels. Bridges, expressways, refinery tank farms, industrial parks, airport runways, and many structures, not shown here, have since been added. From that standpoint, the scene today is greatly altered. This is a transitional view: between what was and what is. (*Philadelphia Maritime Museum*)

139. AFTER ENTERING the Schuylkill River, which means "hidden stream," and passing the Girard Point Bridge, the Girard Point wharves and grain elevator, and finally the Penrose Avenue Bridge, a waterborne observer would find himself approaching Point Breeze soon after he rounded the first major horseshoe in the river. A motorist coming out of Center City Philadelphia is on top of it where Passyunk Avenue crosses the river. It is an area of petroleum storage tanks,

138

refineries, and gas works. From here, on 19 November 1861, two years after Edwin Drake brought in his oil well at Oil Creek in western Pennsylvania, the 224-ton brig *Elizabeth Watts* of Camden, New Jersey, sailed for England with the first full cargo of oil ever shipped overseas from the United States. She arrived at Victoria Docks, London, fifty-one days later with 901 barrels of rock oil and 428 barrels of coal oil. Illustrated in this print, circa 1866, are the Atlantic Petroleum Storage Company's wharves at Point Breeze. *(Philadelphia Maritime Museum: Loan from the J. Welles Henderson Collection)*

140. Within a few years, the Atlantic Refining Company, as it then called itself, had considerably expanded. The brick house with massive end chimneys and signs painted on the side to advertise ships' stores, hardware, tinware, and oils is one of the few features still recognizable from the earlier print. The large building is the company's case and can department; the buildings to the right of the house contained the barreling department. *(Philadelphia Maritime Museum)*

141. A photograph looking in the opposite upriver direction, taken in the early 1900's, captures a sizzling summer day.

The water itself looks oily, and the big four-masted bark in the foreground has an awning rigged over the deck against the heat of the sun. The Point Breeze Gas Works appears in the background. *(City Archives of Philadelphia)*

142. THE Point Breeze Gas Works tanks are visible through the rigging of the unidentified five-masted bark as a Commissioners of Navigation launch, on an inspection tour, approaches the Passyunk Avenue railroad bascule bridge. The

bridge opened upwards in the middle to permit vessels to pass farther upriver. The Reading Railroad's Civil War-vintage tug *Atlantic*, built in 1862, is tied up to a dock at the right. *(Philadelphia Maritime Museum)*

143. THE SECOND BRIDGE farther upstream is Gray's Ferry Bridge, the place where, in April 1789, the citizens of Philadelphia greeted George Washington as he passed through on the way to his inauguration in New York City. A short distance beyond Gray's Ferry, on the east bank at the corner of Bainbridge (Shippen) Street, the Philadelphia Naval Asylum opened its doors in 1831. It was designed by architect William Strickland, whose principal work in Philadelphia had

143

been the U.S. Second Bank and was about to include the Merchants' Exchange. The Naval Asylum also functioned as a government naval school for midshipmen. It was directed by Commodore James Biddle. After the founding of the United States Naval Academy in 1845, the Naval Asylum's instructional functions were transferred to Annapolis, Maryland. Since 1879, the Asylum has been known as the U.S. Naval Home. John L. Gihon's 1856 watercolor records the building and its grounds at that time. *(Philadelphia Maritime Museum)*

144. NAUTICAL TRAINING for Pennsylvanians and Philadelphia area residents did not end forever. Under authority of the state legislature, the Pennsylvania Nautical School was established on 17 April 1889. The purpose was to train boys between the ages of seventeen and twenty to become future officers in the United States Merchant Marine. A thorough classroom schooling in navigation, seamanship, and marine engineering was to be supplemented by practical experience at sea. The U.S. sloop of war *Saratoga* thus became the school's first training ship for the initial eighty-four cadets. Built in 1842, the *Saratoga*'s service had included suppression of the slave trade off the African coast and participation in Commo-

144

dore Matthew Calbraith Perry's "opening" of isolationist Japan in the early 1850's. She was the Nautical School's ship between 1890 and 1907. *(Philadelphia Maritime Museum)*

145. WHEN the training ship *Saratoga* was discovered to be unseaworthy, the Pennsylvania Nautical School arranged with the Navy to replace her with the *Adams,* a combination sail-steam gunboat launched from the Boston Navy Yard in 1876. For several years thereafter, the *Adams* had cruised on the North and South Atlantic Stations, but the majority of her naval service had been in the Pacific. She came to the Nautical School in 1907 from duty as a station ship in Samoa. Until the outbreak of World War I, when the *Adams* was transferred to the New Jersey Naval Militia, the cadets performed annual summer cruises to Europe and winter cruises in the West Indies. *(Philadelphia Maritime Museum)*

146. IN 1919, following the end of World War I, the Pennsylvania Assembly reconstituted the Nautical School. Thereafter, nautical instruction and sea training was to be administered by the Pennsylvania State Board of "Commissioners of Naviga-

146

tion for the River Delaware and its Navigable Tributaries." The new cadet vessel, the *Annapolis,* was a veteran gunboat of the Spanish-American War. Built at Elizabethport, New Jersey, and twenty-four years old, the *Annapolis* sailed in June 1920 from Penn Treaty Park, bound for the West Indies, on her first training cruise. She continued as Pennsylvania's floating school until transferred to the Maritime Commission in April 1940. *(City Archives of Philadelphia)*

147. OLD-FASHIONED square-rigger sea training out of the Delaware River vanished until 1971, when William Wikoff Smith, a local oil executive, yachtsman, and a major benefactor of the Philadelphia Maritime Museum, acquired and presented the *Gazela Primeiro* to the museum. Built in Portugal in 1883, the Portuguese had used this 178-foot barkentine through the year 1969 to fish the Grand Banks off Newfoundland. During the United States' Bicentennial celebrations in 1976, the *Gazela Primeiro* participated in the Tall Ships' Fourth of July parade up the Hudson River. For several seasons, the vessel cruised with students as part of her complement, but stringent insurance and Coast Guard requirements prevented

a continuance of the practice. In October 1981, ownership was transferred to the City of Philadelphia. Now called the *Gazela of Philadelphia*, she is berthed in the Penn's Landing boat basin when not roving the coast as a goodwill ambassador for the city. (*Philadelphia Maritime Museum*)

148. FOUR BLOCKS northeast of the U.S. Naval Home, the east-to-west flow of Spruce Street is interrupted by the Schuylkill River. Today, no maritime activity enlivens their junction on either bank, but W.H. Rease's lithograph of about 1853 demonstrates that such was not always the case. Francis Bacon & Company's Coal Yard on Spruce Street Wharf boasted the ability to load vessels with dispatch "By Steam Power," but the use of steam seems to have been confined to the ramp behind the boiler house. Judging by the coal yard crew working with the cars atop the bins, steam had not entirely invalidated manpower, and the little schooner loading at the end of the wharf may have been in for a long wait. (*Historical Society of Pennsylvania*)

149. UNLIKE the Delaware River face of Philadelphia, which had no connection with the New Jersey side except by ferry

until 1926, the Schuylkill River shores had been spanned by at least one bridge since the time of the American Revolution. Two other bridges appeared soon after the end of that war: at Gray's Ferry and at the Upper Ferry, below Fairmount. Numerous others gradually followed, replaced periodically as the need arose by more substantial structures. The one shown here, while under construction on 19 December 1889, is the 2,404-foot Pratt Truss Deck Walnut Street Bridge. Behind the masts of the two schooners is the Baltimore & Ohio Railroad passenger station. Over it looms the unfinished tower of the new Philadelphia City Hall. *(City Archives of Philadelphia)*

150. ANOTHER PHOTOGRAPH, recording schooners and barks made fast to wharves downriver from the Walnut Street Bridge, was taken between 1893 and 1897 when the photographer, Edward Wanton Smith, was a student at the University of Pennsylvania. *(The Edward W. Smith Collection, Mystic Seaport Museum, Inc., Mystic, CT)*

151. SKETCHED on 28 July 1865 by David J. Kennedy from Walnut Street Wharf, on the west bank of the Schuylkill, the 1,528-foot-long Chestnut Street Bridge, opened in June 1866, rises but has yet to receive its two iron arches. Just upstream can be seen the pylons and trusses of the Market Street Bridge. Navigation for ocean-going ships ended in this vicinity, only barges and scows being able to proceed farther up to the dam under the Fairmount Water Works. By 1930, Philadelphia gloried in 573 bridges, including railroad ones. *(Historical Society of Pennsylvania)*

152. A PONTOON BRIDGE built by the British during the Revolution spanned the Schuylkill at the Middle Ferry, the western foot of High (now Market) Street. French naturalist and artist Charles Alexandre Lesueur made a pencil sketch of one of its successors, the first permanent bridge built across the river. Completed in 1805 as a privately-owned toll bridge, it

151

was widened to accommodate tracks of the Pennsylvania Railroad, but in November 1875 a spark ignited a leaking gas main crossing it, and the bridge was destroyed. A temporary one, built within twenty-one days, followed. A replacement steel cantilever structure completed in 1893 eventually gave way to a two-span bridge opened in 1932. (*American Antiquarian Society*)

153. THE FOCAL POINT of David J. Kennedy's watercolor copy of a Thomas Birch painting is Paul Beck, Jr.'s shot tower, built in 1808 where Twenty-First and Cherry Streets intersect. It is also represented in the previous illustration by Lesueur. Beck, who in 1820 proposed improvements to the Delaware Avenue waterfront but was opposed by Stephen Girard, built his shot tower on the banks of the Schuylkill the same year Thomas Sparks built his beside the Delaware. Beck's square 166-foot-high tower had a daily shot manufacturing capability of five tons, but the venture folded within twenty years. Two shot towers were one too many. (*Historical Society of Pennsylvania*)

154. THE Upper Ferry Bridge at Callowhill/Spring Garden Street began as a primitive, semi-floating structure constructed after the Revolution. It washed away in a spring freshet, was rebuilt, and then washed away again. A more sturdy and permanent bridge, sketched by David J. Kennedy from the second story of Upper Ferry House in 1836, was erected in 1812. Known as the Wernwag Bridge, after its engineer, it was considered a wonder for its beauty and 343-foot single wooden span. Although not clearly delineated by Kennedy, each end was designed with a well-proportioned portico, and thirty windows graced each side of the span. The bridge burned on 1 September 1838. Charles Ellet, Jr.'s famous replacement wire suspension bridge opened 2 January 1842 but was removed in 1875. The heights of Fairmount, containing the City's reservoir, and the accompanying Water Works appear in the background. *(Historical Society of Pennsylvania)*

153

154

155

155. LOOKING UPSTREAM from the Upper Ferry Bridge, the Water Works—as viewed by Thomas Birch in the early 1820's—have changed relatively little from then until now. Lemon Hill Mansion still peers down at the river from its hilltop perch, and water still flows over the dam. But gone are the Schuylkill Navigation Company's canal locks, newly opened when Birch painted this scene, and in their place the West River Drive leads commuters to and from their Center City offices. Gone, too, are the double-sternwheel paddle steamers. So are the big Durham boats, one of which is shown being rowed downstream. Durham boats, ordinarily used to haul coal, grain, timber, and bulk goods from remote rural areas to the metropolis, were the type of craft in which George Washington and the Continental Army crossed the ice-choked Delaware River on Christmas night of 1776 to engage the British at Trenton. *(Pennsylvania Academy of the Fine Arts: Charles Graff Estate Bequest)*

156. FALLING into disuse, the locks of the Schuylkill Navigation Company at Fairmount became overgrown and derelict, used only by weekend fishermen and youthful explorers on an outing. The Callowhill/Spring Garden Street Bridge replacing Ellet's masterpiece can be seen in the distance; the Water Works are just out of the picture plane on the left. The Schuylkill Navigation Company, chartered in 1813, sought to provide easy access to the coal regions further north. As early as 1823, the canal boat *Lady of the Lake* was making connections with mail coaches running between Reading and Philadelphia. In 1841, more than a half-million tons of coal reached the City via the company's system, but ever-expanding railroads soon put the Schuylkill Navigation Company into a decline from which it was never able to recover. *(S. Robert Teitelman Collection)*

157. JAMES CREMER'S 1876 photograph of Centennial Philadelphia viewed from the observatory at Lemon Hill is undoubtedly one of the more striking photographs of its era. Unlike today, not one vehicle travels the road known as East River (Kelly) Drive. The ink-like line crossing the Schuylkill is the waterfall at the dam; between it and the bridge lies an awning-covered, floating bath establishment, popular with swimmers ("bathers") for almost twenty years. Above the Water Works is its Italianate standpipe with the Fairmount reservoir in conspicuous evidence beyond. Fifty years later,

156

The Philadelphia Museum of Art would be constructed on that very site. In the foreground, the clubhouse roofs of the "Schuylkill Navy" sweep towards an excursion boat landing. But, beyond the bridge downriver, the Schuylkill exhibited no such elegance. Gas works had gone into operation in 1836 at Twenty-Third and Market Streets, and industrial waste, sewage, and the flushings of an abattoir on the west bank at Thirtieth and Race were turning the lower Schuylkill into an open cesspool that took generations to reverse. *(Free Library of Philadelphia)*

158. A DELIGHTFULLY classic excursion stern-wheeler—even for 1870, or so, when this photograph was taken—is about to back out of her slip adjacent to the Fairmount Water Works. The *Genl Hooker* was one in a series of steamers to ply the tourist Schuylkill trade. This service apparently began around 1820 and continued for three-quarters of a century, or more. The earliest river schedules were sporadic but sometimes ventured even as far upriver as Norristown, some twenty miles distant. At mid-century, the little steamers began running regular schedules to East Falls and Wissahickon or, farther still, to the mill and manufacturing town of Manayunk. *(Free Library of Philadelphia)*

159. A ROUGHLY comparable view, captured in 1984, testifies to the subsequent blossoming of the rowing clubs along Boat House Row but regrettably does not picture any pleasure steamers above the falls, because they no longer exist. *(Author's Photograph)*

158

159

160

160. Boating came early to the Schuylkill; rowing, rather than sailing, seems to have been favored. Perhaps that happened because the lower Schuylkill, unlike the Delaware, is narrow and winding and so compels a small boat sailor to make constant and frustratingly short tacks. Sailing becomes a mental bore under such conditions, but rowing in a straight line enlivens soul and body. On 21 August 1866, David J. Kennedy sketched Belmont Cottage, below Belmont Mansion and south of the Columbia Railroad bridge. The watercolor's interest is not so much that this was a favored spot for picnics or that the building was demolished in 1881, as he noted, but that an early shell with four rowers and a coxswain is passing the cottage hell-for-leather. *(Historical Society of Pennsylvania)*

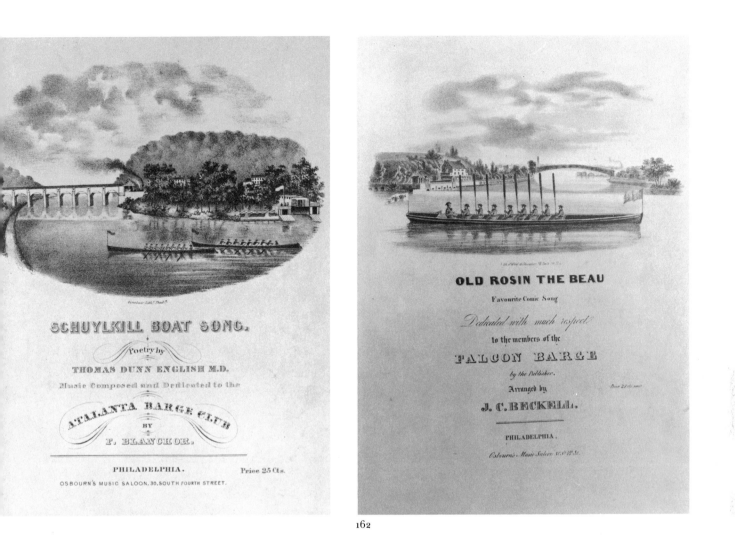

162

161-162. ROWING became a romantic theme in a romantic age, leading to a number of sheet music offerings calculated to dramatize the "Old Boy" spirit. *(S. Robert Teitelman Collection & Philadelphia Maritime Museum)*

163. THOMAS EAKINS not only enjoyed his opportunities to paint tuck-ups racing on the Delaware River or shad fishermen hauling their nets off Gloucester, New Jersey, but he also relished the excuse to capture thrilling moments of a tight sculling race. His "Biglin Brothers Turning the Stake," painted in 1873, is an example. No one knows when the first contest took place on the Schuylkill River, but the locale has become renowned for its devotion to the sport and may fairly be dubbed the "Henley of America." Challenges are known to have been offered as early as 1835. The Bachelors Barge Club, founded in 1853, was followed the next year by the University Barge Club. By 1858, the so-called "Schuylkill Navy" had come into existence. Each spring and autumn, today, rowing crews from schools and universities around the country come to Philadelphia for competitions or to prepare for forthcoming Olympic games. *(Cleveland Museum of Art: Hinman B. Hurlbut)*

164. "Max Schmitt in a Single Scull," 1871, is one of Thomas Eakins' most famous works, showing the champion oarsman, who was also Eakins' high school friend, momentarily resting on his oars as he turns a bend in the Schuylkill and peers over his shoulder to judge his position. The ducks near the point are reminiscent of the huge flocks of Canada geese which today wander the Schuylkill riverbank along Fairmount Park. *(Metropolitan Museum of Art: N. Punnett Fund & Gift of George D. Pratt)*

165. By 1893, the Schuylkill Navy consisted of a dozen clubs and fourteen hundred members, with their quarters ranged along Boat House Row. Within a few more decades, Philadelphia Olympic winners had become almost as numerous as the

163

river geese. The lighthouse, on the end of the most northerly clubhouse, once guided the Schuylkill excursion steamers returning from their evening cruises to Wissahickon or Manayunk. *(Author's Photograph)*

166. MANAYUNK, a strange name to outsiders but of local Lenni Lenape Indian derivation, supposedly meaning "our place of drinking," became a town in 1824, incorporated in 1840, and was absorbed by the City of Philadelphia in 1854. It is the last community of size or importance on the Schuylkill River, within the city limits. Manayunk owes its existence to the Schuylkill Navigation Company. A segment of the old canal survives here and is being restored. A woodcut illustration of 1830 depicts it during its prime. (*Library Company of Philadelphia*)

167. THE WATERPOWER created by the lock and dam attracted mills, factories, and a labor force from the immigrant

piers of Delaware Avenue, whose descendants continue to cherish and inhabit the area. Manayunk grew rapidly, but modern visitors would not fail to recognize it even from this lithograph of about 1850. The Green Lane Bridge connects the east bank of Manayunk with the residential communities of the Main Line. (*Historical Society of Pennsylvania*)

168. IT WAS the looms and manufactories of Manayunk in the northwest, the extraordinarily varied industry of the Great Northeast, and the region's shipyards that once caused Philadelphia to be known as "The Workshop of the World." And, it was the shipyards, from Wilmington on the south to Kensington on the north, that prompted the Delaware River to be dubbed the "American Clyde," after the most famous shipbuilding river of all. Although Philadelphia had shipyards from the beginning, the nicknames did not originate until the latter part of the nineteenth century. It has been estimated that during the interval between the beginning of the Revolution and the United States' Bicentennial year of 1976, Delaware Valley shipyards built 948 naval vessels of all classes, including a few for foreign governments. The period of World War II, alone, accounted for 534. The number of commercial vessels built on the river since 1682 must be staggering. In 1943, Adiel Martin Stern pictured one of the river's longest lived and most productive nineteenth- and twentieth-century fabricators of commercial and naval ships, the "Cramp Yard," about which more will be said further on. (*The Mariner's Museum of Newport News, Virginia*)

168

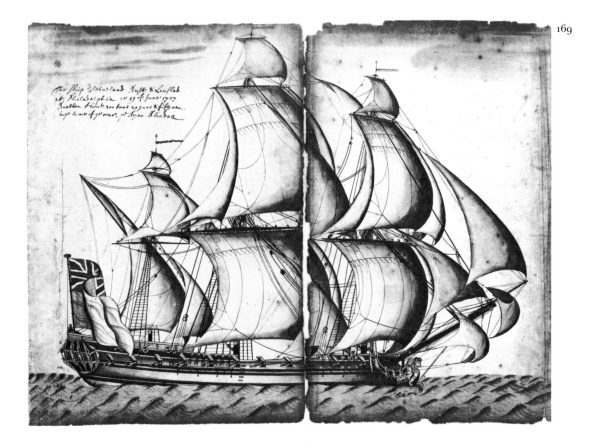

169. A HITHERTO unpublished wash drawing of the ship *Cleaveland* is probably the earliest portrait of a Philadelphia-built ship known. In burden about 300 tons, pierced for twenty guns, and manned by a crew of fifty, this impressive vessel was launched in Philadelphia on 19 June 1707. *(Lancashire Record Office, England)*

170. NOT QUITE a hundred years later, in 1801, another 300-ton vessel, the *Rousseau,* was launched in Philadelphia for Stephen Girard's growing ventures in the China trade. In Edwin H. Lincoln's photograph of 1887 she is the ship closest to the jetty, ending her days as a whaleship sailing out of New Bedford, Massachusetts. *(Peabody Museum of Salem, Massachusetts)*

171. IN STARK CONTRAST to both the *Cleaveland* and the *Rousseau,* a later product of another Delaware River shipyard, the New York Shipbuilding Corporation, was the United States guided missile destroyer *Barney,* launched on 10 December 1960 and shown here under the Walt Whitman Bridge passing seaward during trials. *(Philadelphia Maritime Museum)*

172. NAVAL SHIPBUILDING on the Delaware River began, in effect, as a result of the American Revolution. Philadelphia yards had been building armed merchantmen, privateers, and letters-of-marque throughout the eighteenth century, so the construction of true ships of war was simply an extension of what they already had been doing. In late 1775, the designs for the first twelve frigates of the Continental Navy were prepared in Philadelphia; four frigates and one sloop of war were built here during the war years. Following ratification of the Constitution and after continuous foreign attacks on American vessels abroad, a Federal Navy came into existence. The principal architect for the new navy's first frigates, including the renowned *United States* and *Constitution,* was Philadelphia's Joshua Humphreys. He had been intimately involved with the design of the Continental frigates and was later the United States' first Chief Naval Constructor. His own shipyard, in which several of the early frigates were built, was located in Southwark, on the back doorstep of Gloria Dei (Old Swedes') Church. W.H. Lamb captured the late-eighteenth-century flavor of Humphreys' yard in his recreated scene painted circa 1910. *(Atwater Kent Museum)*

173. THE ONLY KNOWN contemporaneous view of Joshua Humphreys' shipyard is William and Thomas Birch's engraving of 1800, entitled "Preparation for War to defend Com-

merce." On the stocks, the U.S. frigate *Philadelphia* nears completion as the shipwrights lug heavy timbers up the steep incline of the brow. An armed guard stands in his sentry box, alert for trouble, while the foreground figure in a dark coat, believed to represent Humphreys himself, observes the progress. (*Philadelphia Maritime Museum*)

174. GLORIA DEI (Old Swedes') Church looks today very much as it did in Humphreys' time, except that masts no longer tower over it–as seen in this photograph of 1854–and the Delaware River is no longer close enough to lap at its foundations, as it once was. Built between 1698 and 1700, Gloria Dei was a mission of the National Church (Lutheran) of Sweden, but in 1845 the congregation joined the Episcopal Communion. (*Free Library of Philadelphia*)

175. SOON after the launching of the *Philadelphia* from Joshua Humphreys' yard below Christian Street, the Secretary of the Navy acquired land upon which to build a proper Navy Yard, near the foot of Wharton Street, a short distance to the south. Here, from 1815 to 1875, some thirty-five warships were constructed. The most impressive among them, although, as history would demonstrate, the least useful, was the 120-gun

174

ship-of-the-line *Pennsylvania*. She took fifteen years to build and was designed by Humphreys' son Samuel, who succeeded his father as Chief Naval Constructor. When the *Pennsylvania* was finally launched on 18 July 1837, she proved to be not only as unwieldy sailer but already obsolete as a fighting machine. On the day of her launching, nonetheless, the spectator fleet on the Delaware River was unparalleled for its size and enthusiasm, here graphically illustrated by George Lehman. The *Pennsylvania* never got further than the Navy Yard at Norfolk, Virginia, where she remained until 20 April 1861, at which time she was burned to the waterline to prevent her from falling into Confederate hands. *(Philadelphia Maritime Museum: Loan from the J. Welles Henderson Collection)*

176. A LOFTY VIEW of Philadelphia in the late 1830's was taken from the rooftop of the northernmost ship house in the Navy Yard. Many familiar sights are shown, including Sparks' shot tower and, in the far distance to its left, Paul Beck, Jr.'s rival tower on the banks of the Schuylkill. To their right are the heights of Fairmount. More in the foreground, Old Swedes' Church and the site of Humphreys' former shipyard are visible beside Swanson Street, running along the waterfront towards the ship houses. The nearer islands are Windmill and Smith's; that further upstream is Petty's Island, above Camden. *(Philadelphia Maritime Museum: Loan from the J. Welles Henderson Collection)*

177. THE HATCH WINDOWS in the ship house roofs, as well as the ones in the sides, were highly necessary features in the days before electric illumination. The windows in the ends were part of removable panels, which were hinged to swing out of the way or were removed completely during hot weather and whenever a launching was imminent. W.A.K.

176

177

Martin's delightful watercolor of 1859 shows the tall shears used to hoist masts and other heavy items aboard the vessels. The gun carriage shop and foundry appear at the right. *(Gloria Dei [Old Swedes'] Church)*

178

179

180

178-180. DAVID J. KENNEDY also found the Navy Yard and vessels connected with it to be intriguing subjects for his watercolors. This one, painted in 1864, is more atmospheric than documentary but gives a good impression of the facility during Civil War days. While on a sketching expedition in August 1861, he captured an image of the U.S. Receiving Ship *Princeton* moored in the stream opposite the Yard. Her appearance belies the fact that she was a combination steam and sail vessel. A more modern engine of war, sketched by Kennedy off the Navy Yard in 1863, was the rebel ram *Atlanta*, built in Scotland as a screw steamer and blockade runner. The Confederate government took her over in 1862, converted her to a ram at Savannah, and subsequently lost her to Union monitors on 17 June 1863. *(Historical Society of Pennsylvania)*

181. THE Union Volunteer Refreshment Saloon and Hospital, located adjacent to the Navy Yard ship houses, was one of several similiar charitable organizations set up around Philadelphia during the Civil War for the use of Union Troops

181

passing through. Rather like a U.S.O. facility of today, the Refreshment Saloon brought warmth and cheer to otherwise forlorn military men. The hospital offered medical attention that was hard to come by elsewhere. Opened in 1861, the Union Volunteer Refreshment Saloon began in a small boat shop on Swanson Street, south of Washington Avenue, and was the brainchild of a Southwark grocer, Barzilai S. Brown. It expanded gradually as donations of money allowed. Washing accommodations were offered as well as writing rooms where soldiers and sailors could write letters home, franked free of charge. Some 900,000 men, it is said, were furnished with complimentary meals at the Saloon. Edward Moran's painting of 1866 shows four Zouaves carrying a wounded comrade towards the hospital, while white-bearded Samuel B. Fales, Corresponding Secretary & General Financial Agent of the organization, converses with other members of the committee. Fales commissioned the painting. *(Philadelphia Maritime Museum: J. Welles Henderson Collection)*

182. SKETCHING from the deck of the U.S. Receiving Ship *Potomac* on 23 September 1875, David J. Kennedy recorded the beginning of the end for the old Philadelphia Navy Yard. It is "situate[d]," he wrote in his explanatory caption, "on the Delaware River, bounded by Front, Prime, and Wharton Streets. Some of the best and most efficient vessels of war in the United States Navy were built here The dismantle and removal of the Ship Houses &c commenced on September 7th

1875 to the New Navy Yard at League Island, the southern terminus of Broad Street." The old property was disposed of at a public sale held in the Merchants' Exchange: John C. Bullett, representing the Pennsylvania Railroad Company, paid $1,000,000 cash. Pier 55 South Delaware Wharves today occupies the modern waterfront equivalent of the site; the old Navy Yard itself would have been landlocked by the early twentieth-century widening of Delaware Avenue and the riverward thrust of the new bulkhead and pierhead lines. *(Historical Society of Pennsylvania)*

183. PREPARATIONS for the move of the old Navy Yard to League Island, at the junction of the Delaware and Schuylkill Rivers, had already well advanced when David J. Kennedy took stock of the progress on 17 November 1874; "Sketched," he commented, "from top of the Dry-dock at the terminus of South Broad Street with the Delaware River. The wooden bridge is the centre line of Broad Street and leads to the pier and Receiving ship about 100 yards from the sea wall." League Island had been purchased by the City of Philadelphia in 1862 for $310,000; in late 1868, it was presented to the Federal Government for use as a modern, expanded Navy Yard. The final move was made on 7 January 1876. Broad Street south of Moyamensing Avenue at that time was little more than a steep embankment cutting through a swamp. *(Historical Society of Pennsylvania)*

183

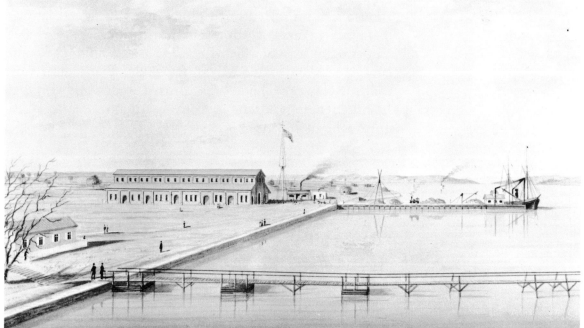

184. "Big Jim," the pulsometer, raises water by steam and atmospheric pressure from behind a dike at League Island on 6 May 1892. Years of work went into creating the new Navy Yard, not the least of which was filling in surrounding swampland, creeks and rivulets. It is no wonder that much of the nearly twenty-two million cubic yards of Smith's and Windmill Island dredgings wound up on or around League Island during the 1890's. *(Atwater Kent Museum)*

185. F. Cresson Schell's turn-of-the-century view of the Navy Yard gives an impression of the activity that daily increased the base's importance. By the time of World War I, it was considered to be the largest facility of its kind in the world.

A 1,030-foot drydock, opened in 1921, similarly was regarded to be without peer. Schell's view looks along Broad Street, behind which the tower of Philadelphia City Hall is silhouetted against the horizon. At the upper left is the Girard Point grain elevator. The entrance to the Schuylkill River appears further left, while a tidal channel flows up behind the Yard, later improved to be used as a reserve basin for decommissioned ships. *(Philadelphia Maritime Museum: Loan from the J. Welles Henderson Collection)*

186. LEAGUE ISLAND is no longer called the "Navy Yard;" it is now, more properly, the Philadelphia Naval Base. It has had many a distinguished visitor over the years. Two of them were photographed in 1929. Secured in a slip at the corner of Broad Street and Delaware Avenue lies the cruiser *Olympia*, launched in 1892 from the Union Iron Works in San Francisco. She became famous as the flagship of Commodore George Dewey during the battle of Manila Bay in 1898. One of her lesser-known honors was to bring home from France, in 1921, the remains of the Unknown Soldier, for interment in Arlington National Cemetery. Today, the *Olympia* is an attraction in the Penn's Landing boat basin. *(City Archives of Philadelphia)*

187. BASKET MASKS still in place, the battleship *Pennsylvania* awaits a two-year League Island overhaul, days after her arrival from Cuban waters. Later damaged during the Japanese

186

air attack on Pearl Harbor, in 1941, she was repaired and subsequently received eight battle stars. The *Pennsylvania* was sunk off Kwajalein Lagoon in the Pacific two years after being used as a target ship during the 1946 Atomic-bomb tests at Bikini Island. *(City Archives of Philadelphia)*

188. A MORE RECENT visitor to the Philadelphia Naval Base was the United States Aircraft Carrier *Saratoga*, pictured here. Her September 1980 arrival at Philadelphia elicited a spectator welcoming fleet of a size unprecedented in years. The first naval vessel of the name *Saratoga* was an eighteen-gun

sloop of war, built in Philadelphia by Joshua Humphreys during the American Revolution. The present aircraft carrier's immediate namesake, another carrier of 1920-1925, had been built on the opposite bank of the Delaware River by the New York Shipbuilding Company, in Camden, New Jersey. During a nearly three-year period, the latest *Saratoga* underwent a thorough reconditioning and modernization, calculated to keep her at sea for another generation. Not long after she vacated her dry dock, it was occupied once again: this time by the U.S. Aircraft Carrier *Forrestal*. *(Philadelphia Maritime Museum: U.S. Navy Photograph)*

189. A NUMBER of townships along the Delaware River or tucked up inside one of its tributary streams once built schooners for the intercoastal trades, big shad skiffs for fishing, or dredgeboats for oystering, but most of their shipyards were small and of limited production. It was the upriver giants who worked around high-pressured schedules and kept the flow of iron and steel moving through their gates at formidable rates of speed. From the middle decades of the nineteenth century through at least World War I, the first of these behemoths were to be encountered at Wilmington, Delaware. Harlan & Hollingsworth and Pusey & Jones are two such shipyards that spring to mind. With equal grace, they turned out anything from vessels of war to *African Queen*-style riverboats to steam yachts of the most palatial dimensions and posh appointments. The accompanying illustration is of the Harlan & Hollingsworth plant during the 1880's. *(Philadelphia Maritime Museum)*

189

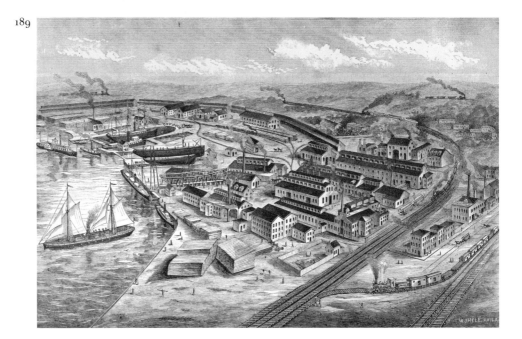

190. HALFWAY between Wilmington and Philadelphia lies Chester, Pennsylvania, settled by the Swedes in the mid-seventeenth century. At Chester, other shipbuilding combinations evolved. Reany, Son & Archbold's yard of 1859 was acquired by John Roach and eventually renamed the Delaware River Iron Shipbuilding & Machine Works, which continued under various guises into the twentieth century. The first vessel built there by Roach was launched in 1872. His yard was part of a conglomeration of enterprises with which he became involved and, by 1885, the yard had constructed more iron vessels than all the other major Delaware River shipyards put together. The first true oil tanker built in America, the *Standard*, for Standard Oil, was constructed here in 1888. As can be seen from an undated photograph, Roach could also work in wood. *(Philadelphia Maritime Museum)*

191. THE TWO ASPECTS of Roach's operation can be seen in a photograph of the yard, again undated. Wooden vessels are under construction at the right, but at the left iron boilers await completion. Note the horse-drawn steam pumper parked on the brink of the jetty. *(Philadelphia Maritime Museum)*

192. A MORE DRAMATIC view of the facility appears in A.C. Stuart's oil painting of the launching of the *City of Washington* on 30 August 1877. Spectators, on the decks of vessels in the foreground, watch as the 300-foot New York and Cuba Mail Steamship Company's liner slides into the Delaware River. As she does, a cannon on the monitor's after-deck fires a congratulatory salute. The letters "FA" on the flag stand for F. Alexandre & Sons, for whom the *City of Washington* was built. *(The Mariner's Museum of Newport News, Virginia)*

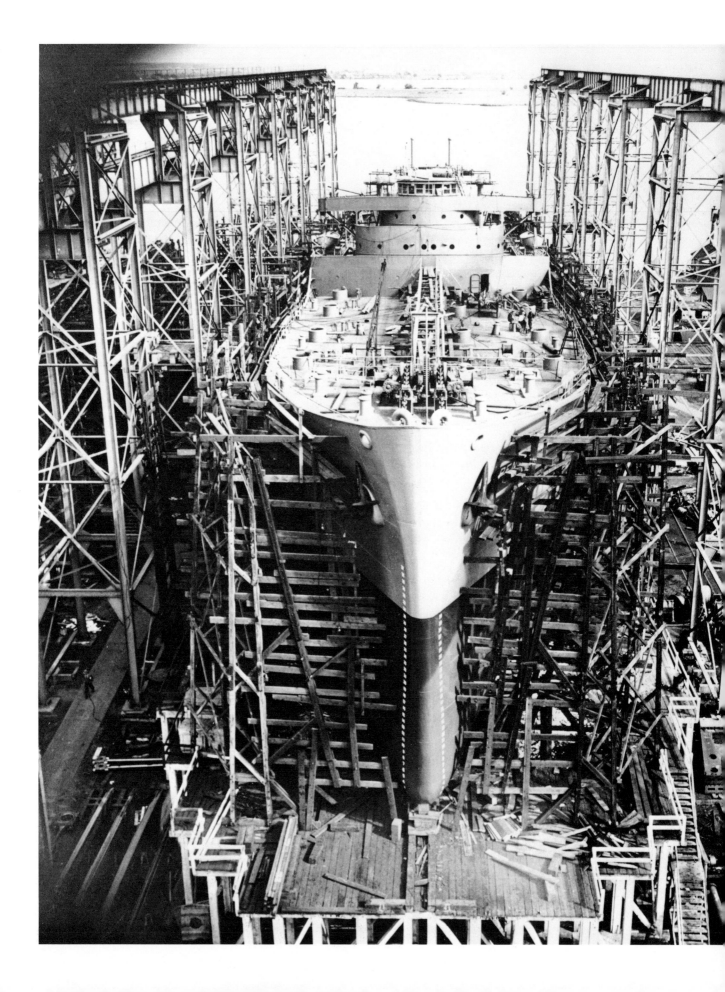

193-194. A LATE COMER to the Chester scene was the Sun Shipbuilding & Dry Dock Company, a subsidiary of the Sun Oil Company and referred to, familiarly, as "Sun Ship." The company launched its first vessel, the S.S. *Chester Sun*, on 30 October 1917. A dramatic 1938 photograph by A. Knott records the later *Pennsylvania Sun* nearing her launch date. Another scene, captured thirty years afterwards, shows the Sun Leasing Company's white-hulled *Ponce de Leon*, a container/roll-on roll-off vessel of 17,597 tons. Next to her lies the not-yet-completed United States Lines' cargo ship *American Legion*. Ironically, one of the U.S. Lines' corporate ancestors, the American Line, was founded at Philadelphia in 1873 to carry freight, mail, and passengers between Philadelphia and Liverpool. (*Philadelphia Maritime Museum*)

195. Between the 1917 launching of the *Chester Sun* and the end of the 1960's, Sun Ship delivered 543 vessels. Its shipyard is pictured here about 1968. During the World War II years, the company produced 281 oil carriers, nearly forty percent of all tankers built in the nation throughout the conflict; twenty-eight slipways were in operation in 1943. Peace brought about a predictable, but drastic, decline in new orders. On 8 February 1982, Sun Ship was taken over by the Pennsylvania Shipbuilding Company. The final outstanding delivery at the time of the transfer was the container/roll-on roll-off *Thomas Heyward*, built for Waterman Steamship Lines. She entered the Delaware River early in 1983. Repair work and conversions now occupy the affairs of Penn Ship. *(Philadelphia Maritime Museum)*

196-197. The largest shipyard anywhere at the end of World War I, and for several years thereafter, was at Hog

Island, Philadelphia, about seven miles upriver from Sun Ship. On 30 May 1919, the Hog Island shipyard launched five vessels in forty-eight minutes and ten seconds. Nothing remains to be seen of it today; the runways of the Philadelphia International Airport have taken its place. Created by the crisis of war, the Hog Island facility was fully built from scratch in less than ten months on some 846 acres of fields and marsh. Fighting still raged in Europe when, on 12 February 1918, the American International Shipbuilding Corporation laid its first keel. At one time, upwards of 300 freight cars a day arrived with prefabricated materials from as far away as Kansas. Fifty shipways, twenty outfitting basins, and 35,000 daily workers made possible the miracles that happened at Hog Island. By the time the post-war recovery ended, the need for new ships had come to a halt, and the plant closed down at the end of January 1921. One hundred twenty-two vessels – "Hog Islanders" – had been completed for the U.S. Shipping Board Emergency Fleet Corporation, a Federal agency. *(Philadelphia Maritime Museum)*

197

198. MASS-PRODUCED, flat-bottomed, straight-sided, possessed of few graces or well-proportioned curves to marvel at, but consistently a chunky 7,500 deadweight tons, "Hog Islanders" would charm the modern eye only for their quaintness. Yet for several generations—until they wore out, sank, or went to the scrapyard—these plain little vessels did good service around the world. The first vessel launched from the yard was the *Quistconck*, the Indian name for Hog Island. She is shown being completed in a fitting out basin. Most Philadelphians have long since forgotten Hog Island or have never known it once existed; this despite the fact—so it is said—that its memory cries out to them daily from thousands of sidewalk window scribblings. The ubiquitous "Hoagie," pronounced "Hoggie" and known elsewhere as a "submarine sandwich," is, supposedly, an enduring relic of World War I "fast food" consumed by shipyard workers between shifts at Hog Island. (*Peabody Museum of Salem, Massachusetts*)

199. PUSEY & JONES Corporation, founded at Wilmington in 1848 to manufacture steam sawmills and engines, completed its first ship in 1853 and continued in business until the late 1940's. After the Civil War, it delivered over one hundred shoal-draft vessels for use in Central and South American

waters. It pioneered in the use of steel plating and profitted in the pre-Great Depression days of the twentieth century by building a number of large power yachts. During the two World Wars it delivered a few minesweepers and fleet auxiliaries. Shown here in 1919 is the Pennsylvania Shipbuilding Company yard, organized and operated by Pusey & Jones, in Gloucester, New Jersey, opposite Philadelphia's Greenwich Point. Fitting out at the right is the 439-foot *Henry Clay,* owned by the U.S. Shipping Board. *(City Archives of Philadelphia)*

200. ONE of the true giants on the Delaware River was the New York Shipbuilding Company (or Corporation), founded in 1899 and active until 1967. Its former yard in South Camden, New Jersey, is still highly visible from the Philadelphia waterfront and is partially used nowadays for the Broadway

Terminal of the South Jersey Port Corporation. A photograph of New York Ship in 1930 shows the heavy cruiser *Chester*, launched a year before, and the stern of the new Grace Lines' Latin American liner *Santa Clara*. The *Chester* received eleven battle stars for World War II service in the Pacific; the *Santa Clara*, under another name, was sunk during the Normandy invasion. New York Shipbuilding Company was organized by a former president of Harlan & Hollingsworth in Wilmington and came to the Delaware River when difficulties arose about building its intended yard on Staten Island, New York. The first keel was laid in 1900: the oil tanker *J.M. Guffey*. During a formidable history and through the two World Wars, New York Ship built cargo vessels, passenger liners, river and harbor craft, dredges, battleships and a host of other naval vessels. *(City Archives of Philadelphia)*

201. Among the more remarkable vessels built in the Camden yards of New York Ship was N.S. *Savannah*, shown here during her launching on 21 July 1959. Mrs. Dwight D. Eisenhower was the sponsor. The *Savannah* was the world's first commercial vessel to be propelled by nuclear power. She had been ordered by the States Marine Lines of the U.S. Department of Commerce's Maritime Adminstration for experimental voyages and worldwide demonstration purposes.

201

Final fitting out and sea trials delayed her maiden voyage until August 1962. The *Savannah*, in addition to cargo, also carried sixty passengers in one class, and thereafter operated primarily between the United States and ports in the Mediterranean. Several years later, management of the ship passed to the First Atomic Ship Transport, Inc. of American Export Isbrandtsen Lines. The ship proved to be unprofitable and was frequently the object of anti-nuclear protest. She was mothballed at Savannah on 10 January 1972. (*Philadelphia Maritime Museum*)

202. AT THE FOOT of Christian Street in Southwark, just a stone's throw upriver from the old Navy Yard, Messrs. J. Simpson and Neill established a shipyard in 1838. David J. Kennedy's 1893 watercolor illustrates the facility's marine railway and sectional floating dry dock as it appeared about mid-nineteenth-century. The partnership, he noted, dissolved in 1861. The dry dock could be pumped clear of water in an hour, and an 1800-ton merchantman could be docked in the same amount of time. Ship repair, as well as ship construction, was always a key component in Philadelphia's economy. Sparks' landmark shot tower appears yet again in the near background. (*Historical Society of Pennsylvania*)

204

203-204. THE SHIPBUILDERS between Kaighn's Point and Cooper's Point in Camden historically have been as busy as anyone and over the years have included such well known names as John H. Dialogue, Wood & Dialogue, John H. Mathis, and Camden Dry Dock and Shipbuilding Company. An undated photograph of an unidentified wooden ship-building yard on Cooper's Point is supplemented by a turn-of-the-century shot of a Camden yard gang posing for their portraits. The tools they hold include a beetle, broad axes and plane, adzes, maul, and an auger. The man at the right, sitting on a frame clamp, is Samuel Courtney Kemble, who laid out several schooners built at the foot of Linden Street. During World War II, the nearby Mathis Shipbuilding Company launched a minesweeper every thirty days. *(S. Robert Teitelman Collection & Philadelphia Maritime Museum)*

205.

205. ALONG Penn Street in the Fishtown section of Philadelphia the Kensington Screw Dock was founded in 1830. Like Simpson & Neill's dry dock downriver, this was a repair facility. W.H. Rease depicted it as it appeared in 1856, including the whale oil works at the right and the whale weathervane atop the flagstaff. *(Philadelphia Maritime Museum: Loan from the J. Welles Henderson Collection)*

206. THE Kensington Drydock Company, near the foot of Palmer Street, was a busy place when it was photographed circa 1915. Docked at the left is the Cuba Distilling Company's molasses tanker *Nelson*, built at Quincy, Massachusetts, in

206.

1912. The steamer in dry dock is the Merchants & Miners Transportation Company's *Persian*, out of Baltimore, formerly the *Tallahassee* and an 1882 product of the Roach shipyard in Chester. The tugboat *Indian*, under her stern, was built in 1897. (*Philadelphia Maritime Museum*)

207. KING of the "American Clyde" was "Cramp's," a fixture on the Delaware River from 1830 to 1927 and again from 1940 to 1946, although latterly under different management. William Cramp & Sons Ship & Engine Building Company, so incorporated in 1872, was located where the Riverside Industrial Park is today, downriver of Port Richmond. From humble beginnings, Cramp's grew and grew, absorbing not only the older I.P. Morris Company but also the Charles Hillman Ship & Engine Building Company next door. In 1895, Cramp's plant covered thirty-two acres of land with river frontage of 1,543 feet and employed 6,000 people. A print of 1872 shows a relatively modest Reconstruction-period plant and the two City Ice Boats built there in 1866 and 1868. (*Philadelphia Maritime Museum*)

208. THE phenomenal expansion of twenty years at Cramp's is obvious in a lithograph of 1892. The vessels seen in it

represent some of those built by the yard. The two berthed on opposite sides of the nearest pier are identified: the white passenger steamer is the Central Railroad of New Jersey's *Monmouth*, built in 1888; the black-hulled *Essex* of 1890 belonged to the Merchants & Miners Transportation Company. Vignettes depict the 1888 gunboat *Yorktown* and the *Morning Light* of 1853, one of very few true clipper ships built in Philadelphia. Cramp's windmill-like floating crane appears in the foreground. *(Philadelphia Maritime Museum: Loan from the J. Welles Henderson Collection)*

209. WHEN not required for use at the shipyard, Cramp's floating crane *Atlas* could be pressed into service elsewhere. With its 130-ton lifting capacity, sixty-foot hoist, and thirty-six-foot boom out-hang, the derrick was ideal for a number of jobs that land-based machines could not handle. The *Atlas* is shown here on an overcast 24 May 1898 helping to set founda-

tion stones for the new Chestnut Street Pier. For the man on the crib-work at the right, something in the water is more curious or interesting than the crane, which is just about to lower a huge granite block into the water. *(City Archives of Philadelphia)*

210. CRAMP'S built a great many vessels during its history for the United States Navy. Here, in an 1889 painting by F. Cresson Schell, the cruiser *Philadelphia* launched in a blaze of flags on 7 September of that year. *(The Mariner's Museum of Newport News, Virginia)*

211. DELAWARE RIVER shipyards occasionally contracted to build naval vessels for foreign governments as well. The precedent was a long-standing one going back to the brig *Hassan Bashaw*, built as a peace offering for the Dey of Algiers at the end of the eighteenth century. In 1898-1899, Cramp's built the cruiser *Variag* for Imperial Russia. Her rain-soaked launching ceremonies on 30 October 1899 have been recaptured from eyewitness accounts in a retrospective watercolor by Paul Karnow. The *Variag* was badly damaged and scuttled during the Russo-Japanese War but was raised by the Japanese, served for a time in their navy, and in 1916 was sold back to Russia. *(Paul Karnow)*

212. THE Delaware River is no longer the "American Clyde," and Philadelphia has shed its "Workshop of the World" image in the post-World War II era. Mills moved off to the Sun Belt. Railway systems atrophied. Expressways and cheap gasoline provided infinite mobilty for industry to make the move into the countryside and for a labor force to follow it. Shopping centers, suburbia, television, mass air travel, leisure time: these were items in a long catalog of previously unknown concepts that encouraged urban hardships throughout the nation. Large areas of Philadelphia were hit hard. Then, another concept emerged: redevelopment. It began in Center City and spread through the historic heart of Philadelphia. Along Delaware Avenue, the old piers from Market Street to South Street were razed to make way for a new waterfront complex to be known as Penn's Landing, shown here in the late 1960's before it began to take on a distinctive form. *(Philadelphia Maritime Museum)*

213. VIEWED AGAIN from the opposite direction, circa 1970, with the Benjamin Franklin Bridge in the foreground and the Walt Whitman Bridge in the distance, Penn's Landing has almost assumed its final shape. It is dominated by a massive boat basin. Delaware Avenue runs alongside it, and ground is being cleared nearby for a sunken stretch of the Delaware Expressway (Route I-95), part of which can be seen in the upper portion of the picture. In the middle, at the far right, are the three Society Hill Towers, designed by I.M. Pei and built in 1962-1964. The curved street just below them is Dock Street, near the foot of which William Penn stepped ashore in 1682. (*Philadelphia Maritime Museum*)

214-215. BY THE LATE 1970's, Penn's Landing had been landscaped. It also contained an ultra-modern, although then still unoccupied, exposition building. One corner of it is visible

in a photograph in April 1984. Beyond is the Benjamin Franklin Bridge as well as the four-masted bark *Moshulu,* built in 1904 and a veteran of the Europe-Cape Horn-Australian grain trade, now a museum ship and restaurant. Other historic vessels lie in the Penn's Landing boat basin: among them the lightship *Barnegat,* the barkentine *Gazela of Philadelphia* (ex *Gazela Primeiro*), the U.S.S *Olympia,* the World War II submarine *Becuna,* and the Philadelphia Maritime Museum's covered barge *Maple,* now known as the "Workshop on the Water" and used as an exhibiting boat shop to teach traditional Delaware River small craft construction techniques. *(Author's Photographs)*

216-217. For a number of years, the Penn's Landing boat basin has been the scene of much activity during warm weather months—boat shows, summer evening concerts, harbor festivals, and visiting vessels of unusual interest. On 17 June 1982, and for a few days thereafter, Penn's Landing recaptured the flavor of the Delaware Avenue waterfront as it routinely appeared seventy years before. Square-rigged training vessels from around the world assembled downriver and paraded up to Philadelphia in commemoration of the City's

216

Three-Hundredth Birthday. The boat basin became a forest of masts, large and small. More than three million people flocked to the area during the dramatic visit of the "Tall Ships." *(Author's Photographs)*

218. THE DEVELOPMENT of Penn's Landing promises to give Philadelphia a striking waterfront identity for generations to come. The Great Plaza, constructed during the mid-1980's at the foot of Walnut and Chestnut Streets, is shown here in the form of a model by its Philadelphia architects, Cope Linder Associates. Pedestrian and vehicular access ramps from the City's historic area conveniently bridge the barriers of Route I-95 and Delaware Avenue. *(Gerald M. Cope; Berry & Homer Photographics, Inc.)*

219. AS THE PUBLIC becomes increasingly aware of Penn's Landing and the residential, commercial, and recreational facilities attendant to it, the port's maritime activities continue to shift away from the old downtown to modern terminals upriver and down. Here, in 1984, the ship *Tapajos*, belonging to Frota Amazonica of Brazil, unloads at one of the old piers along Delaware Avenue, but such sights are quickly disappearing within easy public view from Penn's Landing. *(Author's Photograph)*

220-222. SOME of the older terminals off Delaware Avenue, such as Piers 84-78 South, continue to serve the port regularly, while the massive and nearly adjacent Packer Avenue Marine Terminal, pictured earlier, is an impressive spectacle, especially as viewed – if not necessarily recognized – by countless air travelers making their final approaches into the Philadelphia International Airport. Upriver, beyond Port Richmond and below the Betsy Ross Bridge, the equally impressive Tioga Marine Terminal complex covers 110 acres of highly sophisticated ground. And, beyond the Tacony-Palmyra Bridge, the Northern Shipping Company's 114-acre terminal adds another dimension to the region's vast maritime resources. *(Philadelphia Port Corporation: Stephenson Air Photos)*

LEST ANYONE FORGET that Philadelphia has been – and continues to be – a port of international significance, let him or her leaf through this book. One last reminder: the Ports of Philadelphia, which encompass the shipping facilities from Trenton, New Jersey, to Wilmington, Delaware, currently rank first in total international waterborne commerce on the North Atlantic East Coast and second, after New York, in general cargo tonnage.

SELECT BIBLIOGRAPHY

Alexander, Robert Crozer, *Steamboat for Cape May* (Cape May, NJ: Cape May Geographic Society, 1967).

Annual Reports of the Philadelphia Maritime Exchange, 1879-   .

Baigell, Matthew, *19th-Century Painters of the Delaware Valley* (Trenton, NJ: New Jersey State Museum, 1983).

Baker, William A., "Commercial Shipping and Shipbuilding in the Delaware Valley," *SNAME Spring Meeting Papers* (NY: The Society of Naval Architects and Marine Engineers, 1976).

Beach, John W., *The Cape Henlopen Lighthouse* (Dover, DE: Henlopen Publishing Company, 1970).

Brandt, Francis Burke, *The Majestic Delaware* (Philadelphia: The Brandt and Gummere Company, 1929).

Bray, Maynard, *Mystic Seaport Museum Watercraft* (Mystic, CT: Mystic Seaport Museum, Inc., 1979).

Bunting, W. H., *Steamers, Schooners, Cutters & Sloops* (Boston, MA: Houghton Mifflin Co., 1974).

A Century After: Picturesque Glimpses of Philadelphia and Pennsylvania (Philadelphia: Allen, Lane & Scott & J. W. Lauderbach, 1875).

Chandler, Charles Lyon; Brewington, Marion V.; and Richardson, Edgar P., *Philadelphia, Port of History, 1609-1837* (Philadelphia: Philadelphia Maritime Museum, 1976).

Clement, A. J., *Wilmington, Delaware: Its Productive Industries and Commercial and Maritime Advantages* (Wilmington, DE: The Board of Trade, 1888).

Cox, J. Lee, Jr., *A Preliminary Survey to Analyze the Potential Presence of Submerged Cultural Resources In the Delaware and Susquehanna Rivers* (Harrisburg, PA: Pennsylvania Historical and Museum Commission, 1984).

Dayton, John Wolcott, *Steamboat Days* (NY: Frederick A. Stokes Company, 1925).

Destination Philadelphia [previously, "Ports of Philadelphia"] (Philadelphia: Philadelphia Port Corporation, 1959-1985).

"Auto Producing Equipment is Shipped," August 1962.

"Balch Institute Traces Roots of our Immigrant Heritage," November/December 1983.

"Born in Philadelphia...United States Lines," March/April 1978.

"Camden Ship Repair Company, Inc.," November/December 1980.

"Dredge *Comber*," by Roy Pirritano, Ports of Philadelphia Day, 1975.

"Hog Island Shipyard was the World's Largest," May/June 1980.

"Kocks Heavy Lift/Container Crane," March/April 1979.

"Last Manned Beacon," by Gerald McKelvey, January/February 1975.

"Old Fort Mifflin," by Robert I. Alotta, January/February 1975.

"100-Yr.-Old Mystery of 1st Overseas Oil Shipment Solved," April 1962.

"Philadelphia's Fireboats...Protectors of the Port," May/June 1981.

"Pennsylvania Shipbuilding Co. Fights Hard for Repair Work," November/December 1983.

"Philadelphia in the Ice Age," by John Maass, November/December 1973 and July/August 1981.

"The Philadelphia Maritime Exchange," by James C. Charlton, November/December 1981.

"Piers 3 & 5, History of the Site," March/April 1982.

"Shipbuilding on the Delaware," November/December 1982.

"Sun in Philadelphia Port," Ports of Philadelphia Day, 1975.

"Sun Shipbuilding and Dry Dock Company," September/October 1978.

"Tioga Terminal," March/April 1974.

Dictionary of American Naval Fighting Ships, 8 volumes (Washington, DC: Government Printing Office, 1959–1981).

Dorwart, Jeffery M. and Mackey, Philip English, *Camden County, New Jersey*

1616-1976: A Narrative History (Camden, NJ: Camden County Cultural & Heritage Commission, 1976).

Elliott, Richard V., *Last of the Steamboats* (Cambridge, MD: Tidewater Publishers, 1970).

50 Years (Camden, NJ: New York Shipbuilding Corporation, 1949).

Four Times Panama: A Century of Dredging the American Way, 1867-1967 (Camden, NJ: American Dredging Company, 1967).

Freedley, Edwin T., *Philadelphia and its Manufactures* (Philadelphia: Edward Young, 1858).

Goodrich, Lloyd, *Thomas Eakins* (Cambridge, MA: Harvard University Press for the National Gallery of Art, Washington, DC, 1982).

Hart, Charles W., "Local Landmark Home of the Schuylkill Navy," *Chestnut Hill Local,* 27 September 1984.

Henderson, J. Welles, *Catalogue of a Special Exhibition of the J. Welles Henderson Collection on the Port of Philadelphia* (Salem, MA: Peabody Museum of Salem, 1957).

Hendricks, Gordon, *The Photography of Thomas Eakins* (NY: Grossman Publishers, 1972).

Jackson, Joseph, *Encyclopedia of Philadelphia,* 4 volumes (Harrisburg, PA: The National Historical Association, 1931-1933).

Jackson, Joseph, *Market Street, Philadelphia* (Philadelphia, Joseph Jackson, 1918).

Klein, Esther M., *Fairmount Park, A History and a Guidebook* (Philadelphia: Fairmount Park Commission, 1974).

Lane, Carl D., *American Paddle Steamboats* (NY: Coward-McCann, Inc., 1943).

Lewis, John Frederick, *The Redemption of the Lower Schuylkill* (Philadelphia: The City Parks Association, 1924).

Lewis, John Frederick, *Skating and the Philadelphia Skating Club* (Philadelphia: Philadelphia Skating Club, 1895).

Looney, Robert F., *Old Philadelphia in Early Photographs, 1839-1914* (NY: Dover Publications, Inc., 1976).

Lytle, William M., *Merchant Steam Vessels of the United States 1807-1868* ["The Lytle List"] (Mystic, CT: The Steamship Historical Society of America, 1962).

McCosker, M. J., *The Historical Collection of Insurance Company of North America* (Philadelphia: Insurance Company of North America, 1967).

Morgan, George, *The City of Firsts* (Philadelphia: The Historical Publication Society in Philadelphia, 1928).

Oedel, William T., *Philadelphia Portrait 1682-1982: Catalogue of an Exhibition Celebrating the Three Hundredth Anniversary of Philadelphia* (Philadelphia: The Historical Society of Pennsylvania, 1982).

Philadelphia and its Environs (Philadelphia: J. B. Lippincott & Company, 1872).

Philadelphia City *Directories.*

Philadelphia Collection, occasional catalogues of Frank S. Schwarz & Son, Philadelphia.

Philadelphia Maritime Museum vertical research files and manuscript volumes of Port Records.

Philadelphia: Three Centuries of American Art (Philadelphia: The Philadelphia Museum of Art, 1976).

Phillips, P. Lee, *A Descriptive List of Maps and Views of Philadelphia in the Library of Congress, 1683-1865* (Philadelphia: The Geographical Society of Philadelphia, 1926).

The Port of Philadelphia: Its History, Advantages and Facilities (Philadelphia: Department of Wharves, Docks and Ferries, 1926).

Ports of Philadelphia Waterfront Facilities (Philadelphia: Philadelphia Port Corporation, 1982).

Prowell, George R., *The History of Camden County, New Jersey* (Philadelphia: L. J. Richards & Company, 1886).

Richardson, Edgar P., "Centennial City," *American Heritage,* XXIII, 1, December 1971.

Rivinus, Marion Willis and Biddle, Katharine Hansell, *Lights Along the Delaware* (Philadelphia: Dorrance & Company, 1965).

Rolfs, Donald H., *Under Sail, The Dredgeboats of Delaware Bay: A Pictorial and Maritime History* (Millville, NJ: Wheaton Historical Association, 1971).

Scharf, J. Thomas and Westcott, Thompson, *History of Philadelphia 1609-1884* (Philadelphia: L. H. Everts & Co., 1884).

Siegl, Theodor, *The Thomas Eakins Collection* (Philadelphia: The Philadelphia Museum of Art, 1978).

Slaski, Eugene R., *Poorly Marked and Worse Lighted: Being a History of the Port Wardens of Philadelphia 1766-1907* (Allentown, PA: The Pennsylvania State University, 1980).

Smith, Eugene, *Passenger Ships of the World Past and Present*, 2nd ed. (Boston, MA: George H. Dean, 1978).

Snyder, Frank E. and Guss, Brian H., *The District: A History of the Philadelphia District U. S. Army Corps of Engineers 1866-1971* (Philadelphia: U. S. Army Engineer District, 1974).

Snyder, Martin P., *City of Independence: Views of Philadelphia Before 1800* (NY: Praeger Publishers, 1975).

Souvenir of Roach's Shipyard (NY: U. G. Duffield, 1895).

Sproule, George F., *The Port of Philadelphia, Its Facilities and Advantages* (Harrisburg, PA: Board of Commissioners of Navigation for the River Delaware and its Navigable Tributaries, 1914).

Stanton, Samuel Ward, *Steam Vessels of Chesapeake and Delaware Bays and Rivers* (Upper Montclair, NJ: H. K. Whiting, 1962).

Stokes, I. N. Phelps and Haskell, Daniel C., *American Historical Prints* (NY: New York Public Library, 1933).

Tatum, George B., *Penn's Great Town* (Philadelphia: University of Pennsylvania, 1961).

Taylor, Frank H., ed., *The City of Philadelphia as it Appears in the Year 1893* (Philadelphia: Trades League of Philadelphia, 1893).

Taylor, Frank H., *The Hand Book of the Lower Delaware River* (Philadelphia: The Philadelphia Maritime Exchange, 1895).

Taylor, Frank H. and Schoff, Wilfred H., *The Port and City of Philadelphia* (Philadelphia: 12th International Congress of Navigation, 1912).

Teitelman, S. Robert, *Birch's Views of Philadelphia in 1800 With Photographs of the Sites in 1960 and 1982* (Philadelphia: The Free Library of Philadelphia, 1982).

Thirty-Third Annual Report of the Board of Directors of the Philadelphia Maritime Exchange (Philadelphia: Philadelphia Maritime Exchange, 1908).

Thomas Birch, 1779-1851, Paintings and Drawings (Philadelphia: Philadelphia Maritime Museum, 1966).

Tyler, David Budlong, *The Bay & River Delaware, A Pictorial History* (Cambridge, MD: Cornell Maritime Press, 1955).

Wainwright, Nicholas B., *Paintings and Miniatures at the Historical Society of Pennsylvania* (Philadelphia: The Historical Society of Pennsylvania, 1974).

Wainwright, Nicholas B., *Philadelphia in the Romantic Age of Lithography* (Philadelphia: The Historical Society of Pennsylvania, 1958).

Wainwright, Nicholas B., *The Schuylkill Fishing Company of the State in Schuylkill 1732-1982* (Philadelphia: The Schuylkill Fishing Company, 1982).

Watson, John F., with enlargements by William P. Hazard, *Annals of Philadelphia and Pennsylvania*, 3 volumes (Philadelphia: Edwin S. Stuart, 1884).

Weygandt, Cornelius, *Down Jersey: Folks and Their Jobs, Pine Barrens, Salt Marsh and Sea Islands* (NY: D. Appleton-Century Company, 1940).

Witney, Dudley, *The Lighthouse* (Boston, MA: New York Graphic Society, 1975).

Wolf, Edwin, 2nd, *Philadelphia: Portrait of an American City* (Harrisburg, PA: Stackpole Books, 1975).

INDEX

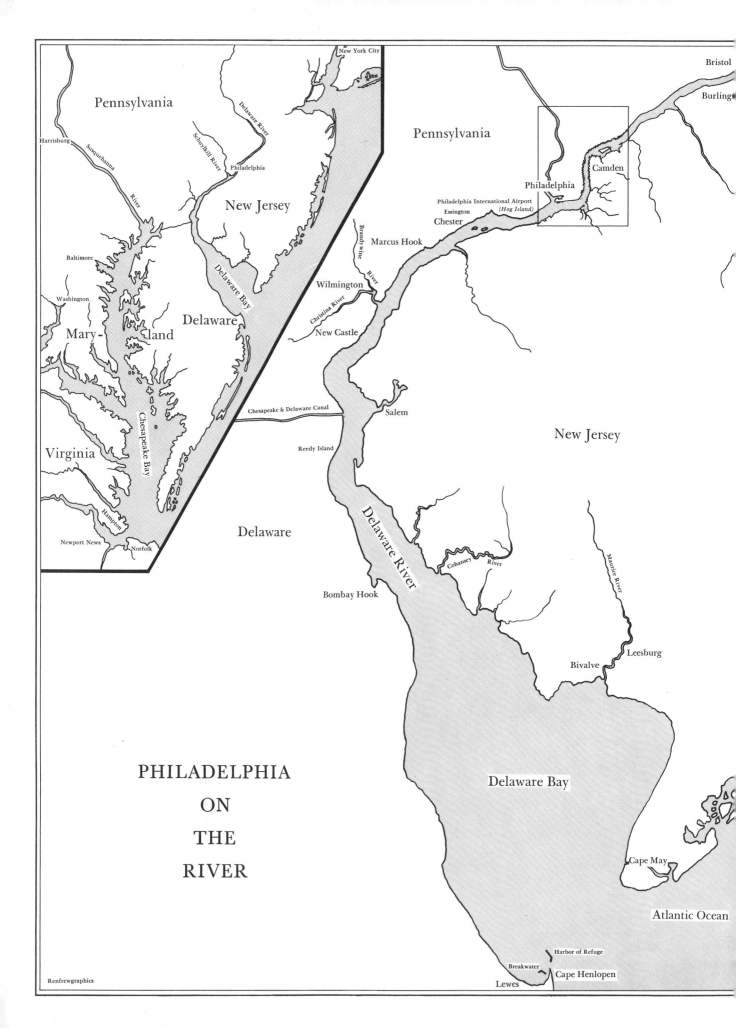

Bristol

Burling

New York City

Pennsylvania

Pennsylvania

Harrisburg

Susquehanna

River

Delaware River

Schuylkill River

Philadelphia

Camden

New Jersey

Philadelphia

Philadelphia International Airport
(Hog Island)

Delaware Bay

Essington

Chester

Baltimore

Marcus Hook

Brandywine

Washington

Delaware

Mary-

land

Wilmington

Christina River

New Castle

River

Salem

Mary-

land

Virginia

Chesapeake Bay

Chesapeake & Delaware Canal

New Jersey

Reedy Island

Delaware

Delaware River

Cohansey   River

Maurice River

Hampton

Newport News

Norfolk

Bombay Hook

Leesburg

Bivalve

PHILADELPHIA

ON

THE

RIVER

Delaware Bay

Cape May

Atlantic Ocean

Harbor of Refuge

Breakwater

Cape Henlopen

Lewes

Renfrewgraphics